# On a Roll to Literacy and More!

Written by:
**Joanne Currah**
**Jane Felling**

1st Printing January 2014

Typeset by Andrea Felling

"Box Cars" won the National Learning Disabilities Association Idea of the Year 1991


ISBN: 978-0-9867131-3-2

# DEDICATION

Dedicated To The Currah Crew

**R** is for Richelle, my right hand girl… really remarkable!

**C** is for Connor, my little commander and a cool character too.

**M** is for Mackenzie, my middle marvel full of magic.

**M** is for Madison, my miniature masterpiece on the move

**C** is for Cameron, who continues to control all chaos as our "charming chief" in charge

You're the Best!

Love, Joanne.

---

*For my number one team;*

*Chris, Andrea and John who,*

*Without a doubt, make it all worthwhile.*

*Love, Jane*

# TABLE OF CONTENTS

# TABLE OF CONTENTS

# INTRODUCTION

We are excited to republish and reformat *On a Roll to Spelling and More (2005)* into *On a Roll to Literacy*. Our new 2013-2014 edition has been updated in name and content to reflect new literacy curriculum. We have made it more teacher friendly with extensive black line masters and have referenced the use of both our unique alphabet dice and letter tiles.

The timing for a newer updated version of our original book has never been better. Listening to teachers and parents around North America, we are constantly asked for ideas to help children with all aspects of literacy. Classrooms and communities are filled with diversity and educators are continuing to look for motivating, hands-on practical game ideas that work. As always, the challenge was to return to our classroom roots to find strategies, tips and ideas to share with our Box Cars fans. From our team at Box Cars, we hope you'll get "rolling" with our updated resources!

# DEAR PARENTS

Dear Parents,

Games are an important part of our overall literacy program in our classroom. Games provide active, hands-on learning opportunities for students each day.

As your child works with the games and activities, they will learn more about letters, letter sounds (phonics), letter-sound relationships, word patterns/families and will discover first-hand how these letter-sound relationships work. This will help your child read and spell even more!

When your child brings home games in their literacy backpacks, we hope that you will find the time to play the games with them. We encourage students to record their work when possible. Most importantly, we want the games to be fun for you both – enjoy!

# WHY GAMES TO TEACH LITERACY?

Games are highly motivating and filled with opportunities to develop many concepts and skills. First and foremost, games generate language and require players to engage in purposeful problem solving and thinking.

It is essential to our philosophy that games provide opportunities for learners to think about a concept as they play. Learners must employ and test out their thinking and strategies and learn from their playing experience. As learners repeatedly engage in challenging games they learn from their mistakes, form generalizations and broaden their understanding of the concept. A good teaching strategy must take into account the various needs of the students, the modes of sensory input (visual, auditory, kinesthetic-tactile) and the cognitive processes involved in literacy. Games incorporate all of a student's senses. They see, hear and touch when they play.

Literacy can be fun and still remain purposeful. We believe it is the special quality of "playfulness" that makes games an invaluable resource to teachers, parents and students.

Before we began the development of the games for this book we reflected on the ways we taught literacy concepts in our classrooms. As we brainstormed the strategies we realized that many of them could form the basis of a game. The rules were written in such a way that a learner can repeatedly practice a concept, skill, rule, mnemonic trick, etc. Within the context of the games experience learners will need to spell, speak, identify and use language effectively.

We also reflected on how language is learned and practiced. Language develops through predictable, sequential stages of development. It can only develop with practise by making successive approximations. In a supportive environment language and literacy become closer to standard, acceptable form. In our games, learners are constantly talking, showing, experimenting and making decisions, verbalizing strategy, and modeling for one another. The opportunity to test out, experiment, make mistakes and learn from that experience enables learners to progress in their development. Most importantly, the games context allows the development to happen with support.

# HOW TO USE THIS BOOK

*On a Roll to Literacy* contains 40 games, extensive variations and reproducible black line masters. Games are organized generally from primary to upper elementary. The table of contents provides a quick reference for suggested grade level and key concepts taught.

All of the games are organized using the following format.

**LEVEL:** Appropriate grade level, intended to be flexible.

**SKILLS:** Specific literacy concepts are listed.

**PLAYERS:** Number needed for playing – intended to be flexible
Competitive, cooperative or solitaire

**EQUIPMENT:** Specific items are listed. New to this updated publication, letter tiles are listed in some games. Any suitable A-Z/a-z cubes, tiles (think Scrabble®), bingo chips marked with letters, etc. can be used. Anything that allows students to manipulate language and provides a multi-sensory learning experience maximizes success.

**GOAL:** How to win

**GETTING STARTED:** Rules and instructions which can be changed to meet individual or group needs.

**VARIATION:** Ideas to increase or decrease difficulty or to change/add a skill.

**TEACHING TIPS:** Some games have Teaching Tips and are identified by this symbol:  Tips will provide specific suggestions for teaching a rule, strategy or concept within the context of that game.

The games do not have to be played in a set order. Teachers and parents can select games to:

1. Introduce a concept or skill
2. Practice a concept or skill
3. Master a concept or skill

Included in this book are simple games that help teach alphabet recognition and initial phonics games that are perfect for developing pre-reading and writing skills. The games begin with opportunities for children to learn the basic phonetic principles and establish correct sound/symbol relationships and rhyming concepts; a perfect place to start for both young and second language learners.

There are extensive games to focus on word beginnings, endings, vowels, common letter combinations, syllabication. Teaching tips are scattered throughout that can be taught with the games.

# HOW TO USE THIS BOOK (CONTINUED)

Children have a natural curiosity about unusual types of words. They are often exposed to rhyme, compound words, homonyms, synonyms and more in their daily literary work. Included are some "unique" games to explore these fun types of words.

For older elementary students and learners wanting an extra challenge – puzzlers brainstormers, pars of speech and advanced games are included at the end of the book. These games may take longer periods of time to complete. They are designed to develop vocabulary, spelling fluency, decision making and logical reasoning. To be successful, students will have to incorporate their understanding of common/probable letter combinations.

# MATERIALS

The strength of *On a Roll to Literacy* is the simplicity of the materials. All that is required to play the games are the following:

1. Alphabet Dice – for classroom use we recommend 1 die per pair or group of students
2. Regular Spotted Dice – 1 pair per child
3. Paper/Pencil or Mini Whiteboards/Marker
4. Reproducible Gameboards – if they are needed it will be specified in the **EQUIPMENT** section of the game rules
5. Alphabet Tiles – players can use these to build words as they play
6. Game Journal – for students to record and save their games, reflect and write about strategies used, concepts practiced, etc.
7. Dictionaries and thesauruses

***ALPHABET TILES:***
To take into account the various needs of students and the modes of sensory input – visual, auditory, kinesthetic – we recommend that alphabet tiles/letters be used during play. Students can roll their letters with the die, take the corresponding letter tiles (a good matching activity in itself), and build words, puzzles, gameboards as they play. The alphabet tiles provide an alternative to paper and pencil practice. The tiles may be moved about easily without the frustration of erasing! Scrabble® letters, magnetic letters, etc. can be used, or specialty letter tiles may be ordered directly from Box Cars at www.boxcarsandoneeyedjacks.com .

# CLASSROOM ORGANIZATION

THE GAMES CLASSROOM IS AN ACTIVE CLASSROOM! The games classroom is a dynamic, interactive place. Students will learn a great deal from talking with one another. Sharing and reflection throughout the games period is an important part of the learning process. When students play there will be lots of talk. Be a good "language detective" and circulate as students are playing. By listening to their talk, teachers often hear evidence of a student's growing understanding of a concept or discover an opportunity to intervene with questions that further develop student understanding.

***ORGANIZATIONAL FORMATS:***

Games can and should be a regular classroom teaching strategy. All students can benefit from consistent playing and practice time. Teachers should implement a schedule that fits both their classroom and timetable needs.

The following organizational suggestions have been shared with us over the years and may provide insight into various classroom implementation formats.

1. A short 10-15 minute playing time is scheduled each day. The first day of the week, the game is taught to the whole group. The group practises over the week to develop and strengthen the concept, skills or strategy of the game. This is often coupled with No.2

2. A longer 30-50 minute game block is scheduled once a week. The game is learned and practised for a sustained playing time. Follow up play periods are offered during center time or free time.

3. Try cross graded practise with a "buddy classroom". Many teachers pair two different leveled classes, i.e. 2 and 4, 3 and 6, etc. for a 30-50 minute game block once a week. The benefits include peer teaching and modeling, improved self-esteem and continued development of language and spelling concepts.

# DISAPPEARING ALPHABET

**LEVEL:** pre-kindergarten and up

**SKILLS:** letter recognition

**PLAYERS:** solitaire or 2

**EQUIPMENT:** one thirty-sided alphabet die, gameboard (see black line master), pencil

**GOAL:** to be the first player to cross off all the letters in the alphabet

## GETTING STARTED:

Player One rolls the alphabet die, and crosses the corresponding letter off of their gameboard. Player Two rolls the die, and crosses the corresponding letter off of their gameboard. Players alternate turns until one player has no letters left on their gameboard. If a player rolls a ☆ the player may choose any letter to cross off.

## VARIATION I:

To increase the difficulty, have players verbalize the sound of the letter and/or a word that begins or ends with the letter, i.e., Player One rolls an S. They cross this off their gameboard and verbalize "sandwich" or "dress".

## VARIATION II:

Instead of crossing off letters, use letter tiles and cover up letters as they are rolled.

---

## *TEACHING TIP:*

Have children print the letter in the air, or trace this letter onto their palm or their partner's back.

---

# DISAPPEARING ALPHABET

| | | | | | | | | |
|---|---|---|---|---|---|---|---|---|
| a | <u>b</u> | c | <u>d</u> | e | f | g | h | i |
| j | k | l | m | <u>n</u> | o | <u>p</u> | q | r |
| s | t | <u>u</u> | v | <u>w</u> | x | y | <u>z</u> | |

| | | | | | | | | |
|---|---|---|---|---|---|---|---|---|
| A | B | C | D | E | F | G | H | I |
| J | K | L | <u>M</u> | <u>N</u> | O | P | Q | R |
| S | T | U | V | <u>W</u> | X | Y | <u>Z</u> | |

# FROM A TO ZEE

**LEVEL:** pre-kindergarten and up

**SKILLS:** printing upper and lower case letters

**PLAYERS:** solitaire or 2

**EQUIPMENT:** one thirty-sided alphabet die, gameboard (see black line master), pencil

**GOAL:** to build the alphabet from A to Z, or from a to z

## GETTING STARTED:

Each player needs a gameboard. Choose either the lower or upper case variation. Player One rolls the die and records this letter in the appropriate space. If a player rolls a ☆, that player may choose any letter to print on their gameboard. If a player rolls a letter previously rolled, the next player proceeds. The first player to correctly fill in their alphabet gameboard is the winner.

## VARIATION I:

To increase the difficulty, have players verbalize the sound of the letter and/or a word that begins or ends with the letter, i.e., Player One rolls an S. They cross this off their gameboard and verbalize "sandwich" or "dress".

## VARIATION II:

Instead of crossing off letters, use letter tiles instead and cover up letters as they are rolled.

---

### *TEACHING TIP:*

After the child records their letter, have them close their eyes and visualize that letter in their favourite colour.

---

# FROM A TO ZEE

| | | | | | | | | |
|---|---|---|---|---|---|---|---|---|
| a | b | c | d | e | f | g | h | i |
| | | | | | | | | |
| j | k | l | m | n | o | p | q | r |
| | | | | | | | | |
| s | t | u | v | w | x | y | z | |
| | | | | | | | | |

| | | | | | | | | |
|---|---|---|---|---|---|---|---|---|
| A | B | C | D | E | F | G | H | I |
| | | | | | | | | |
| J | K | L | M | N | O | P | Q | R |
| | | | | | | | | |
| S | T | U | V | W | X | Y | Z | |
| | | | | | | | | |

# ABC BINGO

**LEVEL:** grade 1 and up

**SKILLS:** letter recognition

**PLAYERS:** 2 - 4

**EQUIPMENT:** one thirty-sided alphabet die, blank gameboard (see black line master), letter tiles (if available) or coloured bingo chips, paper and pencil

**GOAL:** to be the first player to cover four letters in a row horizontally, vertically, or diagonally

## GETTING STARTED:

Players take turns rolling the die, verbalizing the letter rolled, and filling this letter into any blank square of their choice on their gameboard. When all twenty squares have been filled, players are now ready to begin play.

Player One rolls the die and verbalizes the letter rolled. If the letter rolled is a letter that was previously recorded on their board, that player covers this square(s) with their tile(s) or crosses it off. Players take turns rolling the die and covering a square(s). If a letter rolled is not on the board, the next player rolls. If a ☆ is rolled, the player may choose any letter. The first player to complete a row wins.

## VARIATION I:

The winner must also verbalize out loud the sound of each letter.

## VARIATION II:

Before covering squares with their tiles, players must verbalize a word that begins or ends with this letter

---

## *TEACHING TIP:*

This game could be played on mini-whiteboards. Have students create a grid with twenty spaces and stick the letter tiles straight to the board.

---

# ABC BINGO

## GAME 1

| | | | |
|---|---|---|---|
| | | | |
| | | | |
| | | | |
| | | | |

## GAME 2

| | | | |
|---|---|---|---|
| | | | |
| | | | |
| | | | |
| | | | |

# BINGO BLASTERS

**LEVEL:** kindergarten – grade 1

**SKILLS:** letter recognition, sound/symbol

**PLAYERS:** 2

**EQUIPMENT:** one thirty-sided alphabet die, one gameboard per player (see black line master), letter tiles (if available) or bingo chips.

**GOAL:** to be the first player to cover five squares in a row

## GETTING STARTED:

Each player has their own thirty-squared letter Bingo Blaster card. Player One begins by rolling their alphabet die and verbalizing the name of the letter. They may cover this letter with a letter tile or a bingo chip. If a ☆ is rolled, they may cover any square of their choice.

Player Two now rolls a letter, identifies the letter rolled, and covers it with a letter tile on their own gameboard. Players continue to alternate turns. If a letter rolled is already covered, that player misses a turn and their opponent proceeds. The winner is the first player to cover five squares in a row horizontally, vertically, or diagonally.

## VARIATION:

The player must also spell a word beginning or ending with the letter rolled before this letter can be covered.

# BINGO BLASTERS

| | | | | | |
|---|---|---|---|---|---|
| A | B | ☆ | C | D | E |
| ☆ | F | G | H | I | ☆ |
| J | K | L | M | N | O |
| P | ☆ | Q | R | S | T |
| U | V | W | X | Y | Z |

| | | | | | |
|---|---|---|---|---|---|
| a | b | ☆ | c | d | e |
| ☆ | f | g | h | i | ☆ |
| j | k | l | m | n | o |
| p | ☆ | q | r | s | t |
| u | v | w | x | y | z |

# STAND UP

**LEVEL:** kindergarten and up

**SKILLS:** letter recognition, letter printing, initial consonants, vowel sounds

**PLAYERS:** small groups or whole class

**EQUIPMENT:** one thirty-sided alphabet die, paper and pencil

**GOAL:** to be the first player to cross off all five secret letters

## GETTING STARTED:

Each player secretly records five different letters on their paper. One player is selected to be the designated roller for their group. This player rolls and calls out the letter and its corresponding sound. When a letter called out appears on a player's list, that player crosses this letter off their list. Players continue listening for letters and crossing off any letters rolled until one player crosses off all five letters. This player then stands up and is the winner of that round. If a ☆ is rolled, the die is re-rolled.

## VARIATION I:

When the player stands up, that player must also verbalize five words that begin or end with their five letters, i.e., s, h, m, r and o

"snakes, horses, mice, rabbits, owls"

## VARIATION II:

To increase the difficulty, players may also spell their five words, and earn 1 point for each correctly spelled word.

## VARIATION III:

To practice sentence construction, players must stand up, verbalize words beginning with their five letters, and use all five words to create a meaningful sentence. i.e.:

"Snakes, horses, mice, rabbits and owls can all be found in the zoo."

# ALPHABETICAL ROLL

**LEVEL:** grade 1 and up

**SKILLS:** letter sequencing, alphabetizing

**PLAYERS:** 2

**EQUIPMENT:** one thirty-sided alphabet die

**GOAL:** to be the first player to earn 10 points

## GETTING STARTED:

Player One rolls the die and calls the letter rolled out loud. They also verbalize in sequence the next three letters that follow that letter in the alphabet, i.e., Player One rolls an F and verbalizes "F…G…H…I". If the player is correct, one point is earned. If a player rolls a ☆ , they may choose any letter and name the three letters that follow (exceptions are Y and Z). Players alternate turns until one player earns 10 points and is declared the winner.

## VARIATION I:

The players roll the alphabet die and must name the three letters that precede the letter rolled i.e., M is rolled and the player verbalizes "J…K…L".

## VARIATION II:

After the player names the next three letters in alphabetical sequence, they must verbalize a word that begins with each letter, i.e., N is rolled, the player verbalizes "O…P…Q" and the words "Open, Popcorn, Quietly".

## VARIATION III:

Players extend **variation II** by challenging each other to alphabetize and create words that fit into a specific category (see categories on p. 59).

i.e., Player One rolls a "C" for Countries or Cities, rolls an "N" for their starting letter, and verbalizes "Nigeria, Ottawa, Paris, Quebec"

# RHYMING SNAPPERS

**LEVEL:** grade 1 and up

**SKILLS:** identifying rhyming pairs

**PLAYERS:** 2

**EQUIPMENT:** one thirty-sided alphabet die

**GOAL:** to earn points by verbalizing rhyming pairs

## GETTING STARTED:

Player One rolls the die, and both players identify the starting letter. Both players try to be the first to give a rhyming pair. One of the words must start with the letter rolled. If a ☆ is rolled, the die is re-rolled.

***EXAMPLE:***
Player One rolls a B

Player Two verbalizes "Bag/Rag" and earns 1 point. Players may earn additional points by spelling their words, or by identifying the "rhyming chunk" "ag".

Players alternate rolling the die. After a set period of time, the player with the most points is the winner.

## VARIATION:

To increase the level of difficulty, the players must name three or four rhyming words and/or spell them out loud.

i.e., Roll = N

"Nice, rice, twice and slice",
or
"New, drew, stew and flew" would all be acceptable answers

---

## *TEACHING TIP:*

There are many word families that share the same sound-symbol pattern (phonogram). "Rhyming families" are great to work on to establish early success in spelling.

***EXAMPLE:***

cow/now
low/bow/row

See p.14 for more phonogram examples.

# WORD RACE

**LEVEL:** kindergarten and up

**SKILLS:** creating 3 letter words, ending sounds, middle sounds

**PLAYERS:** solitaire or 2

**EQUIPMENT:** one thirty-sided alphabet die, one sound gameboard per player (see black line master for suggestions), letter tiles (if available) or pencil

**GOAL:** to fill in all the blanks in one or all rows of the gameboard

## GETTING STARTED:

Players alternate rolling the die and filling in letters on their gameboard. Players fill in the spaces that are open and try to create correctly spelled words. Players are allowed a total of 5 reject rolls throughout the course of the game. Only one space may be filled in for each roll. If a ☆ is rolled players may select a letter of their choice. If a vowel is rolled a player may re-roll. Players keep rolling until one player has filled in all of the spaces in one or all rows of their gameboard. The player who has created the most correctly spelled words is the winner.

## VARIATION I:

Players may allow 4- or 5-letter words to be created for extra points, i.e.,

rice
rink
ripe
rich

To create words containing blends or digraphs with more than three letters, players must roll one letter at a time.

## VARIATION II:

When using letter tiles, players may choose to move a tile instead of picking one when a ☆ is rolled. This may be especially useful when playing with 4- or 5-letter words.

## VARIATION III:

Using the blank template provided in the black line master on p.14, players must make their own gameboards before starting play.

# WORD RACE

| | | |
|---|---|---|
| ra__ | su__ | pa__ |
| ru__ | sa__ | pu__ |
| re__ | se__ | pe__ |
| ri__ | si__ | pi__ |
| ro__ | so__ | po__ |

| | | |
|---|---|---|
| __ent | __ash | __ur |
| __ing | __ack | __ate |
| __ock | __un | __ap |
| __id | __unk | __ow |
| __ice | __ub | __ike |

# WORD RACE

| | | |
|---|---|---|
| | | |
| | | |
| | | |
| | | |
| | | |

## PHONOGRAM SUGGESTIONS

| | | | | | | | |
|---|---|---|---|---|---|---|---|
| ack | an | aw | est | ill | oke | ough | ump |
| ad | and | ay | et | in | og | ound | un |
| ail | ank | eat | ice | ine | old | ow | unk |
| ain | ap | ed | ick | ing | ook | oy | up |
| ake | ar | ell | id | ink | or | ub | ur |
| ale | ash | er | ide | ip | op | uck | |
| all | at | en | ight | it | ore | ug | |
| ame | ate | ent | ike | ock | ot | um | |

# VOWEL CROSSES

**LEVEL:** grade 1 and up

**SKILLS:** spelling simple 3 letter words

**PLAYERS:** 2

**EQUIPMENT:** one thirty-sided alphabet die, one gameboard per player (see black line master), letter tiles (if available) or pencil.

**GOAL:** to fill in the gameboard with as many correctly spelled words as possible.

## GETTING STARTED:

Players alternate rolling the die and calling the letters out loud. If a player rolls a ☆ they may choose a letter of their choice.

A total of thirty rolls will be taken during the game. Throughout the rolling, players may place the letters into any space on their gameboard. Any roll may be rejected by either player and placed into the reject spaces. Once a letter is placed into any space, it cannot be moved or changed. After thirty rolls are completed, players count up the number of correctly spelled three-letter words. The player with the most correctly spelled words is the winner

## VARIATION:

To increase the difficulty, players may alter the gameboard to include various double vowel combinations (see p.18 for a blank board).

# VOWEL CROSSES

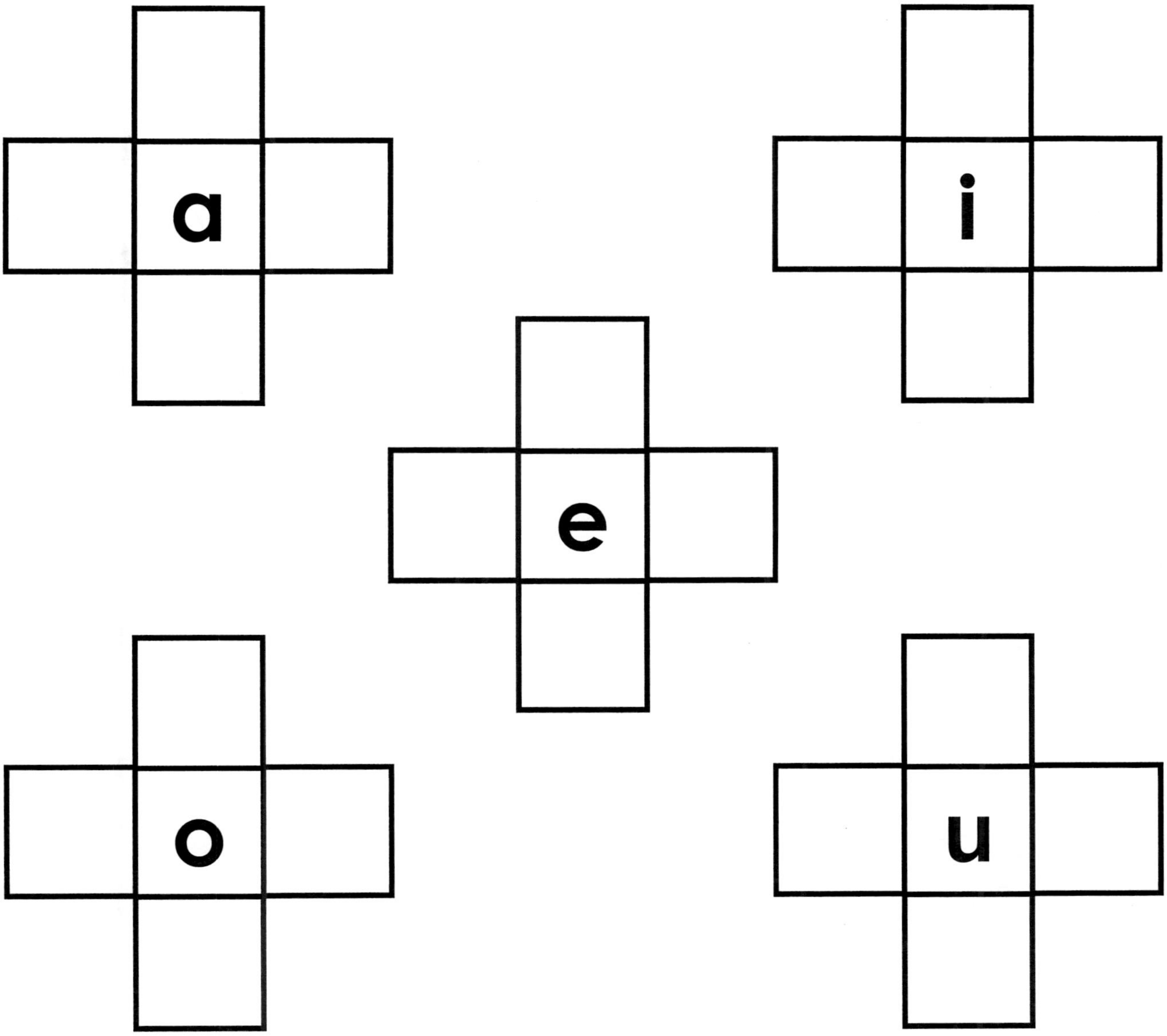


## REJECT ROLLS

| | | | | |
|---|---|---|---|---|
| | | | | |

# VOWEL CROSSES

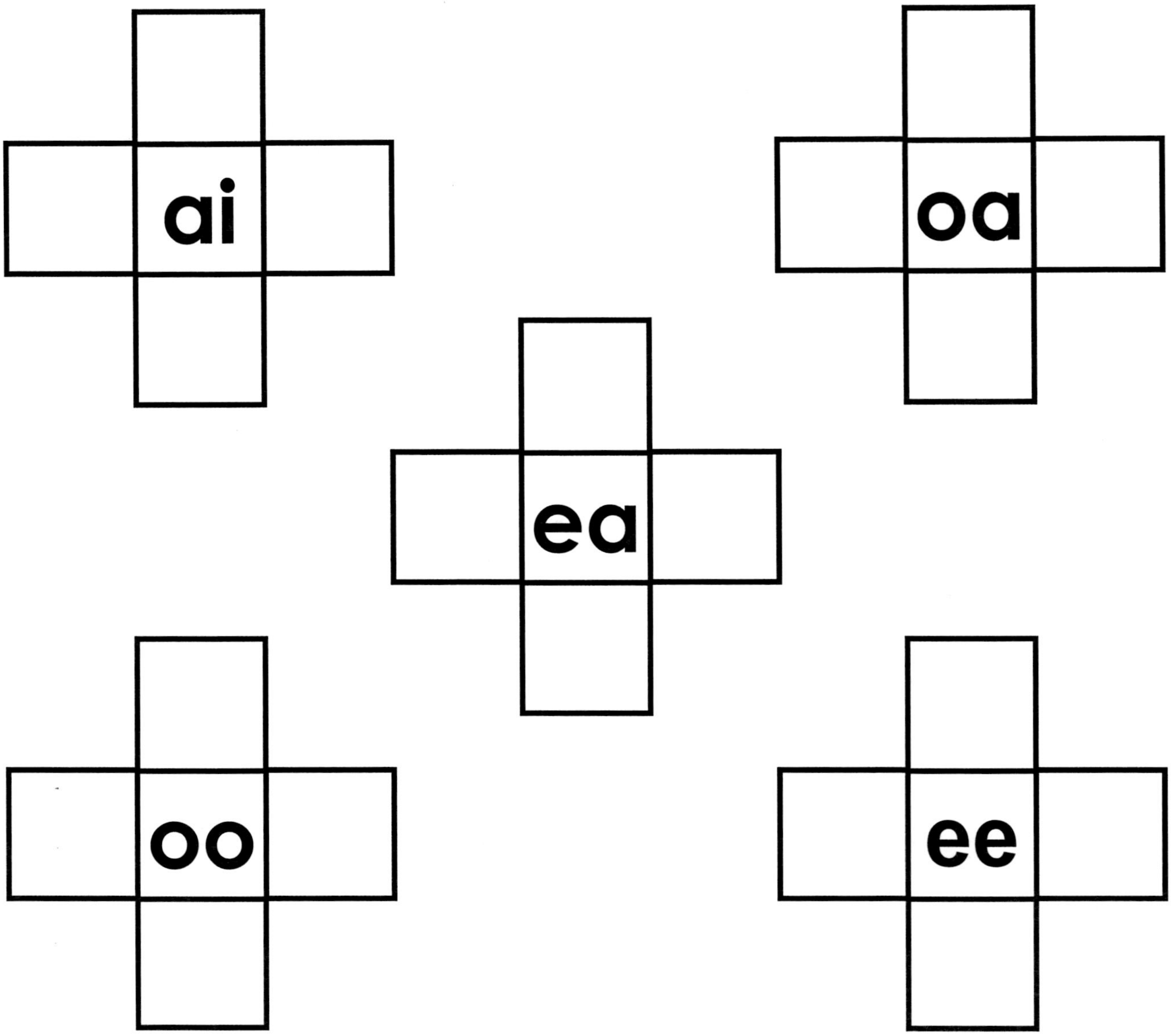


## REJECT ROLLS

| | | | | |
|---|---|---|---|---|
| | | | | |

# VOWEL CROSSES

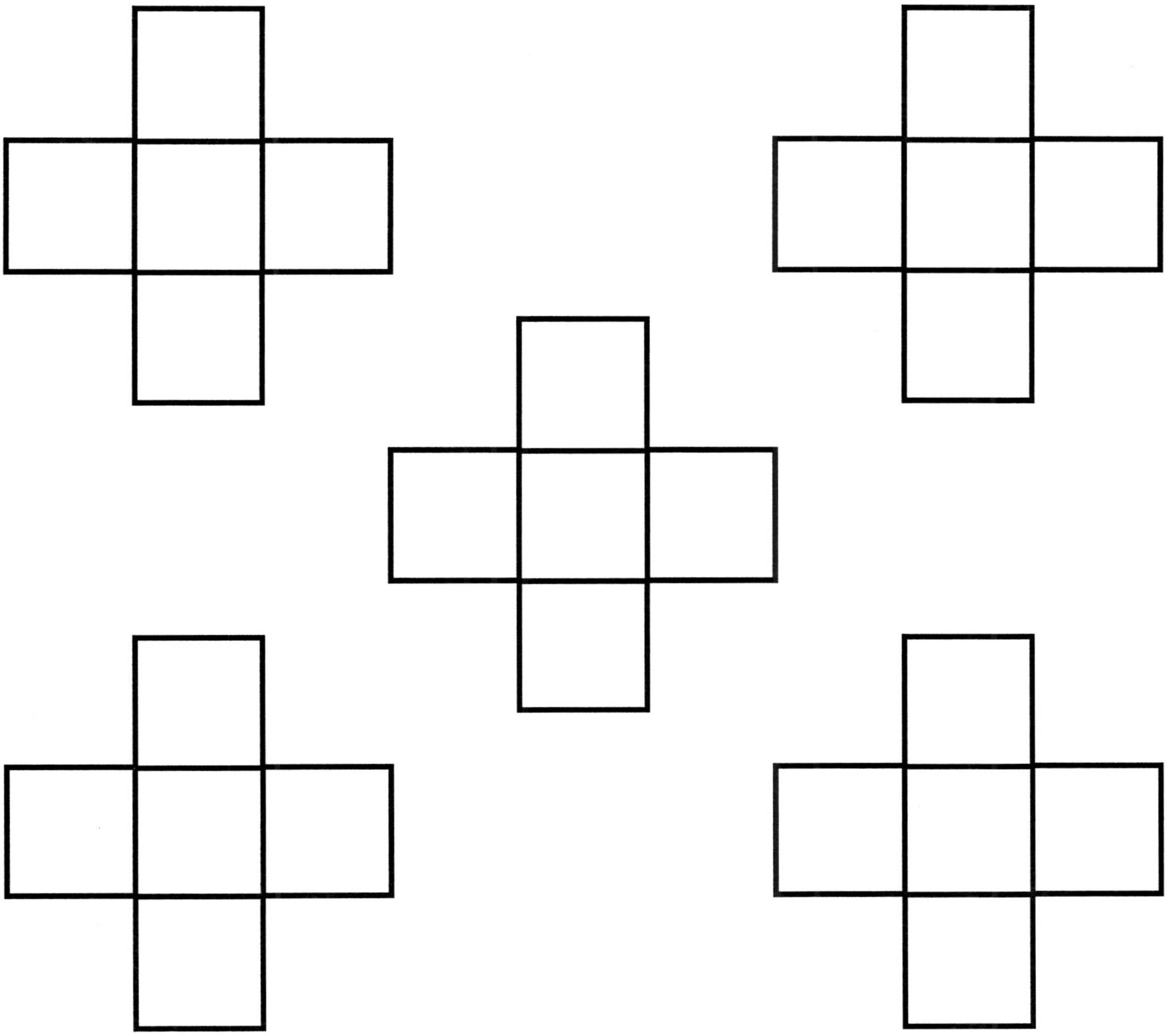

## REJECT ROLLS

| | | | | |
|---|---|---|---|---|
| | | | | |

# UP TO YOUR NECK IN WORDS

**LEVEL:** grade 1 and up

**SKILLS:** spelling simple words

**PLAYERS:** 2 or more

**EQUIPMENT:** one thirty-sided alphabet die, one gameboard per player (see black line master), pencil

**GOAL:** to fill in all the spaces on the gameboard with correctly spelled words

## GETTING STARTED:

Player One rolls the die, identifies the letter and spells a simple word starting with this letter. The player prints this word in the appropriate space on their gameboard. Players alternate turns rolling the die and filling in their gameboard. The spaces do not need to be filled in sequentially.

If a ☆ is rolled the player may choose any letter to record. The first player to fill in all spaces with correctly spelled words on their gameboard is the winner.

***EXAMPLE:***

| | |
|---|---|
| e | end |
| d | dad |
| c | cup |
| b | bed |
| a | and |

etc.
a to z

## VARIATION:

For older students, words can be scored at 1 point per letter, i.e. ball = 4 points, cabbage = 7 points, etc. Calculators may be used to figure out final scores.

# UP TO YOUR NECK IN WORDS

| | Player One | | Player Two |
|---|---|---|---|
| z | ______________ | z | ______________ |
| y | ______________ | y | ______________ |
| x | isn't for anything | x | isn't for anything |
| w | ______________ | w | ______________ |
| v | ______________ | v | ______________ |
| u | ______________ | u | ______________ |
| t | ______________ | t | ______________ |
| s | ______________ | s | ______________ |
| r | ______________ | r | ______________ |
| q | ______________ | q | ______________ |
| p | ______________ | p | ______________ |
| o | ______________ | o | ______________ |
| n | ______________ | n | ______________ |
| m | ______________ | m | ______________ |
| l | ______________ | l | ______________ |
| k | ______________ | k | ______________ |
| j | ______________ | j | ______________ |
| i | ______________ | i | ______________ |
| h | ______________ | h | ______________ |
| g | ______________ | g | ______________ |
| f | ______________ | f | ______________ |
| e | ______________ | e | ______________ |
| d | ______________ | d | ______________ |
| c | ______________ | c | ______________ |
| b | ______________ | b | ______________ |
| a | ______________ | a | ______________ |

# BEG-ENDERS

**LEVEL:** grade 2 and up

**SKILLS:** spelling simple words

**PLAYERS:** 2

**EQUIPMENT:** one thirty-sided alphabet die, letter tiles (if available) or paper and pencil

**GOAL:** to be the first player to correctly spell a word that begins and ends with the established letters

## GETTING STARTED:

To begin, the die is rolled to establish the starting letter, and a second time to establish the ending letter i.e., M is the starting letter and T is the ending letter. Players now alternate rolling the die and recording each letter. The player rolling has the first chance at spelling a word that fits the established criteria. If a player cannot make and spell a word on their roll, they pass and let their opponent have a try. If neither player can spell a word, the next player rolls the die and records another letter. If a ☆ is rolled, the player may select any letter of their choice.

***EXAMPLE:***
Roll = M – start and T – end

Player One rolls D pass Player Two pass

Player Two rolls W pass Player One pass

Player One rolls J pass Player Two pass

Player Two rolls A and spells MAT and scores 3 points (1 point per letter)

Players alternate starting each new round. The player with the most points after a set number of rounds is the winner.

## VARIATION I:

To decrease the difficulty, players roll beginning and ending letters and verbalize any word beginning and ending with these letters to earn a point. Double points are earned for correctly spelling the word.

## VARIATION II:

To increase the difficulty, players refer to the categories on p.59 and roll the alphabet die to select the category for that round. Players then proceed to play "Beg-Enders" with the challenge of creating a word that also fits into the selected category.

# RACE TO SPELL

**LEVEL:** grade 2 and up

**SKILLS:** spelling 2-, 3-, 4- and 5- letter words

**PLAYERS:** 2 or teams of 2 vs. 2

**EQUIPMENT:** one thirty-sided alphabet die, paper and pencil, letter tiles (if available)

**GOAL:** to be the first to spot correctly spelled 2-, 3-, 4-, and 5-letter words

## GETTING STARTED:

Each player needs their own paper and pencil to record the letters rolled. The goal of the game is to be the first player to make a 2-letter word, 3-letter word, 4-letter word and so on (plurals do not count).

Player One rolls the die and all players record this letter on their paper. Players alternate rolling the die and recording the letters. Repeat letters are also recorded. If a ☆ is rolled, the roller may select a letter of their choice.

When any player notices a combination of letters that spell a 2-letter word, they say "Spell It" and spell their word. If they are correct, they score 2 points (one point per letter). Play continues with the next roll. Players now try to find a 3-letter word (worth 3 points) and so on.

Play continues until a 4- and 5-letter word have been created. Players total their points for the round. A new roller is selected for the second round. Play continues for a set period of time. The player or team with the most points is the winner.

***EXAMPLE:***

Player One rolls T

Player Two rolls K

Player One rolls R

Player Two rolls A, ⟶ Player One says "Spell It" and spells "at" for 2 points

Player One rolls P, ⟶ Player Two says "Spell It" and spells "rat" for 3 points

Player Two rolls Q, ⟶ Player Two says "Spell It" and spells "trap" for 4 points

Player One rolls ☆, picks C ⟶ Player One says "Spell It and spells "track" for 5 points

The game is over, as a five letter word has been found. Both players have earned 7 points, and the round is a tie.

# ALPHABET ROLL OUT

**LEVEL:** grade 2 and up

**SKILLS:** spelling simple words

**PLAYERS:** teams of 2 vs. 2

**EQUIPMENT:** one thirty-sided alphabet die, gameboard (see black line master), letter tiles (if available) or pencil, dictionaries are optional.

**GOAL:** to spell the most words with one half of the alphabet

## GETTING STARTED:

***SETUP:***
Before starting the game, teams divide the alphabet letters between both teams. At the end of this setup, each team will have 13 different letters of the alphabet assigned to them. These letters will be used in the spelling portion of the game.

If using letter tiles, a full alphabet is placed face up between both teams. Alternating turns, each team selects one letter tile at a time and puts it onto their playing side. Once each team has all 13 of their letters, the spelling portion of the game can begin.

If not using letter tiles, teams place one written alphabet in the center of the play area. Alternating turns, each team selects one letter, crosses it off the master alphabet and records it on their playing sheet.

***SPELLING:***
Teams now have ten minutes to create as many 2-, 3-, 4- and 5-letter words etc. using their own 13 letter bank.

***SCORING:***
At the end of the set spelling time, players exchange lists to check for spelling accuracy. Dictionaries may be used to double check for accuracy. Words score one point for each letter. Final scores are determined, and the team with the most points is the winner.

# ALPHABET ROLL OUT

| | | | | | | | | | | | | |
|---|---|---|---|---|---|---|---|---|---|---|---|---|
| a | b | c | d | e | f | g | h | i | j | k | l | m |
| n | o | p | q | r | s | t | u | v | w | x | y | z |

Teams select one letter at a time

Record your 13 letters

| | | | | | | |
|---|---|---|---|---|---|---|
| | | | | | | |
| | | | | | | |

| 2-letter words | 3-letter words | 4-letter words | 5-letter words | 6-letter words and longer |
|---|---|---|---|---|
| | | | | |
| | | | | |
| | | | | |
| | | | | |
| | | | | |
| | | | | |
| | | | | |
| | | | | |
| | | | | |

# MEMORY WORDS

**LEVEL:** grade 2 and up

**SKILLS:** spelling simple words

**PLAYERS:** 3

**EQUIPMENT:** one thirty-sided alphabet die, paper and pencil

**GOAL:** to correctly spell words using memorized letters

## GETTING STARTED:

One player is selected to be the recorder for the round, and the other two players will be the rollers. These two players alternate rolling and naming the letters rolled. The recorder prints the letters out of view of the other two players as they are rolled. The other two players must remember the letters rolled. Players attempt to say a word that is spelled with some or all of the letters that have been previously rolled. When a ☆ is rolled, the die is re-rolled.

After a player calls out a word that contains some or all of the rolled letters, the recorder checks for accuracy. The player must spell the word correctly and the recorder verifies that the letters have in fact been rolled. If the player is correct, 1 point is earned and a new round of play begins.

***EXAMPLE:***
Letters rolled in sequence are as follows:
c y r l a d

The following would be acceptable words:
card yard lard car lay day lad ray

If both players call out the same or different words at the same time and both words are accepted by the recorder, then both players earn 1 point. Play continues until one player earns 5 points. This player then becomes the recorder for the next round.

## VARIATION:

Before play begins, players may determine the minimum number of letters per word i.e., only 4-letter words or more are accepted.

---

### *TEACHING TIP:*

Children need many opportunities to practice using their auditory memory as in the above game. In this game, we have players chant back through the letters rolled, silently i.e., “inside their heads” after each new roll.

---

# A MITT FULL OF VOWELS

**LEVEL:** grade 2 and up

**SKILLS:** identifying vowels, spelling simple words

**PLAYERS:** 2

**EQUIPMENT:** one thirty-sided alphabet die, one vowel die or regular die, paper and pencil

**GOAL:** To correctly spell a word containing the vowel indicated on the vowel or regular die and the starting letter indicated on the alphabet die.

## GETTING STARTED:

If using a regular die to generate the vowels, players use the following code:

| | |
|---|---|
| Roll 1 = A | Roll 4 = O |
| Roll 2 = E | Roll 5 = U |
| Roll 3 = I | Roll 6 = Y or Roll Again |

Player One begins by rolling both dice and identifying the starting letter on the alphabet die and the vowel to be used. If a ☆ is rolled, the player may select any letter of their choice

***EXAMPLE:***
Roll = P and 3 (which equals P and I).

Player One spells PITCH. Player One scores 1 point per letter. In this example, Player One would earn 5 points. Player Two now takes their turn. Players continue to alternate turns. The first player to score 100 points is the winner.

## VARIATION:

Concentrate on *long* or *short* vowels only.

---

## *TEACHING TIP:*

TEACH THE RULE: All words, all syllables have at least one vowel!

In any of the simple spelling games, have children trace and draw a shape around their word. Have them visualize this shape when spelling the word a second time. i.e.

pitch

---

# VOWEL DOUBLE DUTCH

**LEVEL:** grade 2 and up

**SKILLS:** spelling simple words containing double vowels

**PLAYERS:** 2

**EQUIPMENT:** one thirty-sided alphabet die, two vowel dice or regular dice, paper and pencil

**GOAL:** to be the first player to correctly spell a word with the corresponding starting letter and vowels.

## GETTING STARTED:

Play begins by rolling both vowel or regular dice. The alphabet die determines the starting letter for the word, and the vowel or regular dice determine which vowels must be used. Players should use their discretion and reroll should an improbable double vowel combination occur, i.e. uu (rarely used, except vacuum). When using regular dice, use the following legend to determine the vowel:

| | |
|---|---|
| Roll 1 = A | Roll 4 = O |
| Roll 2 = E | Roll 5 = U |
| Roll 3 = I | Roll 6 = Y or Roll Again |

***EXAMPLE:***

Player One rolls S, 4 and 5 (which equals S, O and U).

Players must think of and spell an "ou" word staring with the letter S. Some possible answers include: "soup, source and sound".

Player Two rolls B, 3 and 1 (which equals B, E and A).

Players must think of and spell an "ea" word starting with the letter B. Some possible answers include: "beast, beat, bean and beard".

The first player to correctly spell an appropriate word scores a point. The dice are re-rolled for the next round. If a ☆ is rolled, the roller may select any letter of their choice. Play continues for a set period of time. The player with the most points is the winner. At the end of the game, words can be collected and categorized by vowel combinations.

# IT'S ALL IN A WORD

**LEVEL:** grade 3 and up

**SKILLS:** spelling simple to complex words

**PLAYERS:** teams of 2 vs. 2

**EQUIPMENT:** one thirty-sided alphabet die, two regular dice, paper and pencil

**GOAL:** to be the first team to correctly spell a word that contains the letter indicated by the roll of the die

## GETTING STARTED:

One player rolls the dice, and both teams identify the letter. If a ☆ is rolled, players may select any letter of their choice. This letter must be used in the spelled word. Teams next identify how many times this letter must appear in the word. Teams may choose to either add or subtract the dice to determine the quantity. Doubles are automatically a re-roll except for double 1's.

***EXAMPLE:***
Roll = D and 5/3

Team Two spells SADDLE (they chose to subtract 5 – 3 = 2 and used two D's in their word).

The first team to print an acceptable word scores 1 point. The first team to earn 10 points is the winning team

---

## *TEACHING TIP:*

Pronunciation is very important to spelling. Have children slow down and pronunciate each syllable carefully, i.e. <u>To</u> <u>mor</u> <u>row</u> making sure to represent each sound. Every syllable needs a vowel.

---

# POSITIONS PLEASE

**LEVEL:** grade 3 and up

**SKILLS:** spelling complex words, letter position

**PLAYERS:** teams of 2 vs. 2

**EQUIPMENT:** one thirty-sided alphabet die, one regular die, timer, paper and pencil

**GOAL:** to correctly spell words with the rolled letter in the correct position.

## GETTING STARTED:

Team One rolls both dice. The regular die indicates the ordinal position that the letter indicated on the alphabet die must be positioned. If a ☆ is rolled, the die is re-rolled. Both teams have from one to three minutes to spell a suitable word. Teams must now spell a word that matches the roll, i.e. a word with W in the fifth position. This word may begin with any letter.

***EXAMPLE:***
Roll = W and 5. Team One spells "screws" and Team Two spells "thrown".

Teams score 1 point per letter for their correctly spelled word. In the example above, both teams would earn 6 points.

Team Two now rolls the dice for the next round. Play continues until one team earns 75 points.

## VARIATION:

Teams may spell as many words as possible in the given time period. Score 1 point per letter and play to 200 points.

i.e. Team One creates and spells correctly:

screws
software
sidewalk

Team One earns 22 points.

---

## *TEACHING TIP:*

Having students construct their own mnemonic tricks will help them learn tricky or difficult spellings, especially homonyms.

Examples: a piece of pie; a friend to the end; too contains too many o's; a seal in the sea; the principal is your pal

---

# FIT IN THREE

**LEVEL:** grade 4 and up

**SKILLS:** spelling 3-letter words and larger

**PLAYERS:** 2 or teams of 2 vs. 2

**EQUIPMENT:** one thirty-sided alphabet die, paper and pencil

**GOAL:** to correctly spell words containing the three letters rolled by your opponent.

## GETTING STARTED:

Player One rolls the die three times. Each letter is recorded by Player Two. Player Two must correctly spell words (any length) containing the three letters within the established time limit (three to five minutes). Correctly spelled words earn a player 1 point per letter.

***EXAMPLE:***

Roll = T, A and L. Team Two spells TALENT and scores 6 points, ALERT and scores 5 points for a total of 11 points. Other acceptable answers may include, later, tall, lantern, etc.

After the allotted time is over, the players reverse roles. Player Two now rolls the die and Player One spells as many words as possible that include all three letters rolled.

If a ☆ is rolled, the spelling player may select any letter of their choice. Play continues for a set period of time. The player with the most points is the winner.

## VARIATION I:

COMPETITIVE PLAY – The die is rolled three times and letters are recorded. The first player to spell a word containing the three letters scores 1 point per letter. The dice are then re-rolled for round two.

## VARIATION II:

The die is rolled three times and letters are recorded. Both teams or players create as many words as possible during the allotted time. The player or team with the most correctly spelled words earns 1 point.

---

### *TEACHING TIP:*

To speed up play, Team Two can establish their letters and length of words to be spelled at the same time as Team One. Both teams may work on their words at the same time.

---

# SUCCESSFUL SYLLABLES

**LEVEL:** grade 4 and up

**SKILLS:** spelling multi-syllable words

**PLAYERS:** 2

**EQUIPMENT:** one thirty-sided alphabet die, one regular die, paper and pencil

**GOAL:** to correctly spell a word with the correct number of syllables starting with the letter indicated on the alphabet die

## GETTING STARTED:

Players roll both dice and refer to the following legend for the game:

| | |
|---|---|
| Roll = 1-2 | spell a one syllable word |
| Roll = 3-4 | spell a two syllable word |
| Roll = 5-6 | spell a three or more syllable word |

Player One rolls the dice and determines the starting letter and the number of syllables for their word. If a ☆ is rolled, the die is re-rolled. Player has a set time limit (one to three minutes) to correctly spell and/or record their word. If the player is correct then they score 1 point per syllable. Players continue to alternate turns. After a set number of rounds, the player with the most points is the winner

***EXAMPLE:***

Roll = 3 and M. The player must spell a two syllable word starting with the letter M.

"Money, marry, movie" would all be acceptable responses, and the player would earn 2 points.

## VARIATION I:

Allow players to verbalize as many correct answers as possible during the allotted time, and the players earn 1 point for each correct response.

## VARIATION II:

Play a speed variation with three players. One player is the roller, and the other two players race to be the first player to respond correctly to earn a point. Players take turns being the roller.

---

## *TEACHING TIP:*

Teach the concept: Every syllable has a vowel. For a two syllable word ending in the sound "ē", it's usually a y. For example: funny, many, baby.

---

# DICE TOSS CHALLENGERS

**LEVEL:** grade 4 and up

**SKILLS:** spelling up to twelve letter words

**PLAYERS:** teams of 2 vs. 2

**EQUIPMENT:** one thirty-sided alphabet die, two regular dice, paper and pencil, letter tiles (if available)

**GOAL:** to correctly spell words beginning with the letter rolled within the time limit

## GETTING STARTED:

Team One begins by rolling the alphabet die to determine the first letter for spelling. Team Two rolls the 2 regular dice to determine the length of the word Team One must spell, i.e. rolls M on the alphabet die and 4+3 on the regular dice: 4 + 3 = 7. Team One must correctly spell a 7-letter word beginning with the letter M within the established time limit (three to five minutes). Correctly spelled words earn the team 1 point per letter. i.e. Team One would earn 7 points for correctly spelling "magpies".

Teams now reverse roles and team two now has their turn spelling. If a ☆ is rolled, the spelling team can select the starting letter.

Some roll combinations may be next to impossible. i.e. a 2-letter word starting with Q or X. Teams should use their discretion and re-roll when appropriate.

Play continues for a set period of time. The team with the most points is the winner.

## VARIATION:

COMPETITIVE PLAY – Both the alphabet die and the regular dice are rolled at the same time. Both teams now race to be the first to correctly spell a word of the correct length and starting letter.

---

### *TEACHING TIP:*

To speed up play, Team Two can establish their letter and length of word to be spelled at the same time as Team One. Both teams may work on their words at the same time.

---

# RACE TO RHYME

**LEVEL:** grade 2 and up

**SKILLS:** identifying and spelling rhyming words

**PLAYERS:** 2 – 4

**EQUIPMENT:** one thirty-sided alphabet die, paper and pencil, letter tiles (if available)

**GOAL:** to be the first player to make at least two rhyming words

## GETTING STARTED:

Each player needs their own paper and pencil to record the letters rolled. Player One rolls the die and all players record this letter on their paper. Players alternate turns rolling the die and recording the letters onto their paper. Repeat letters are also recorded. If a ☆ is rolled, the roller may choose a letter of their choice which is also recorded by all players.

When one player notices a combination of letters that spell at least two words that rhyme, they say "rhymers". The player must correctly spell the two words in order to earn a point. Play continues for a set period of time. If players say "rhymers" at the same time, then both players must secretly record their rhyming pair. Players share their words. If the pairs are different and spelled correctly, both players earn 1 point each. If the pairs are the same, neither player earns a point and play continues. Players continue to build rhyming words and earn a point for each new pair of "rhymers" The player with the most points at the end of the game is the winner.

***EXAMPLE:***
Letters rolled include: b, f, r, c, j, and a. Player One says "rhymers" and verbalizes "bar and far" and spells them out loud. Player One earns 1 point and a new round of play begins.

## VARIATION:

Extra points can be earned for any additional rhyming words that are found.

bar/far and car/jar

The original pair = 1 point and the additional words earn 1 point each.

---

## *TEACHING TIP:*

If players are using letter tiles, encourage them to stack their rhymes.
***EXAMPLE:*** [j][a][r] stack another tile, "b" on top [b][a][r] to make the rhyme.

---

# WORD SHAPES

**LEVEL:** grade 1 – 3

**SKILLS:** spelling by using word configuration

**PLAYERS:** 2

**EQUIPMENT:** one thirty-sided alphabet die, one gameboard per player (see black line master), letter tiles (if available) or pencil

**GOAL:** to be the first player to fill in the gameboard with correctly spelled words

## GETTING STARTED:

Players need to know and recognize the following terms:

| | | |
|---|---|---|
| Upstairs letters → | ☆ t w o | b d f h k l t |
| Main floor letters → | ☆ m y | a c e i m n o r s u v w x z |
| Basement letters → | ☆ g o | g j p q y |

Players alternate rolling the die and calling the letters out loud. Both players may choose to use any letter and place it into any space in their gameboard. Players may reject ten rolls along the way. The rejected rolls are placed in the appropriate spaces on the gameboard. If a player rolls a ☆ players may select any letter of their choice. Once a letter is in a space, it cannot be changed or erased. Players must only place appropriate letters into the appropriate shaped spaces.

Both players need to continue to roll until all their spaces are filled in. The player with the most correctly spelled words is the winner

## VARIATION:

Play a "Speed Up" variation of word shapes. Players alternate rolling and filling in their shapes until one player has created five correctly spelled words and verbalizes "Word Shapes". This player earns 5 points for that round.

## *TEACHING TIP:*

Having the shape drawn around the word can help some children visualize the word and connect it to the appropriate letters.

# WORD SHAPES

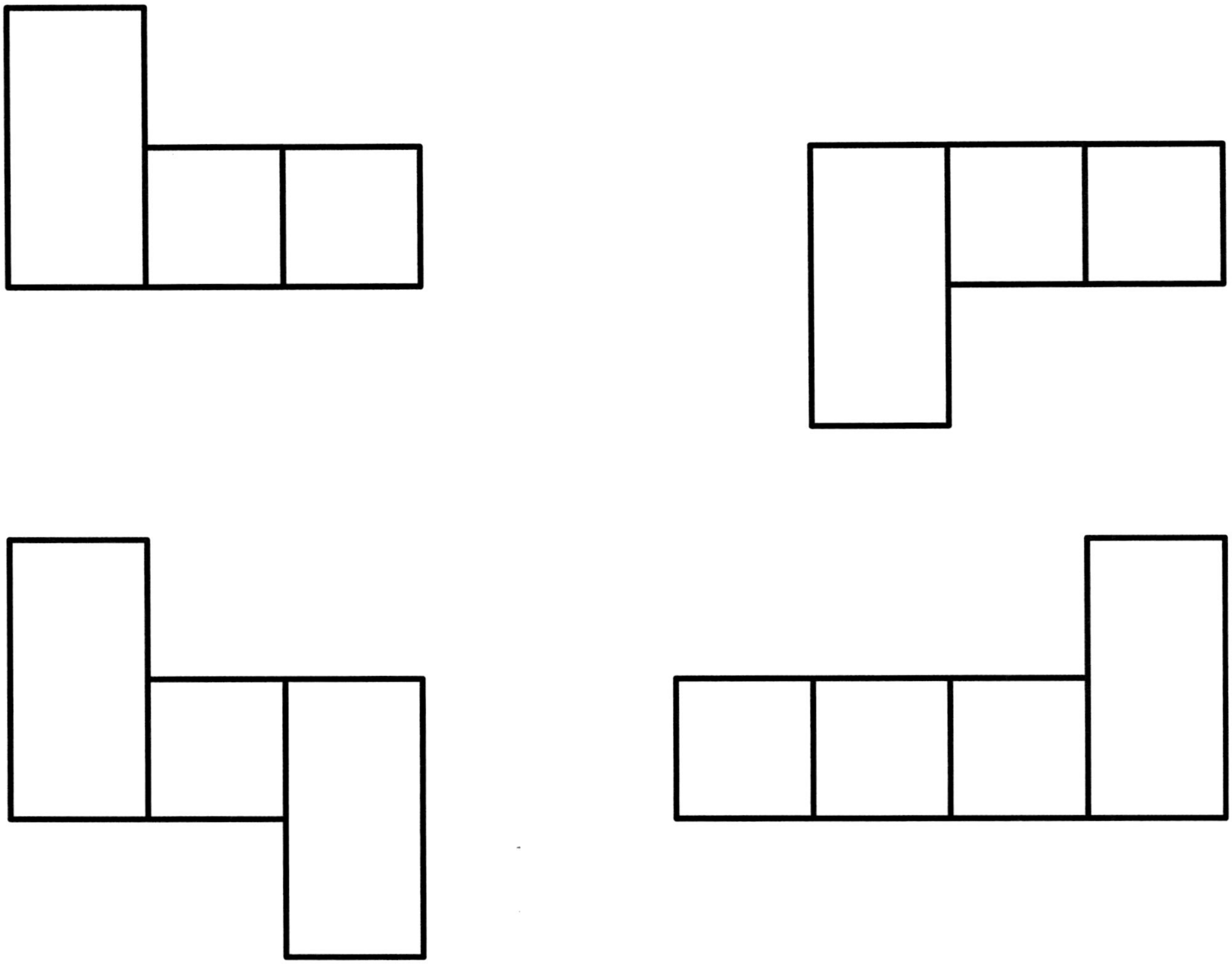

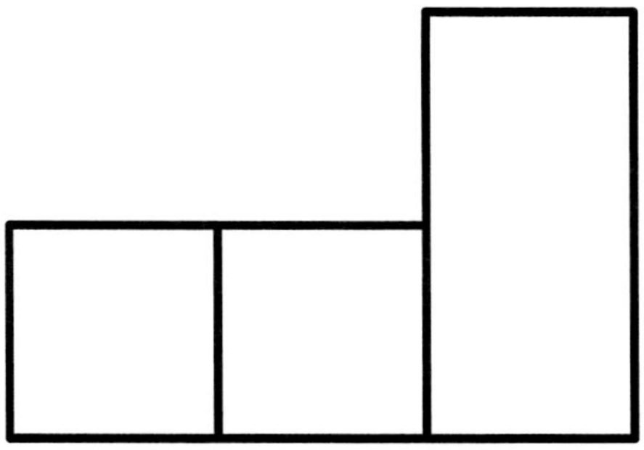

**REJECT ROLLS**

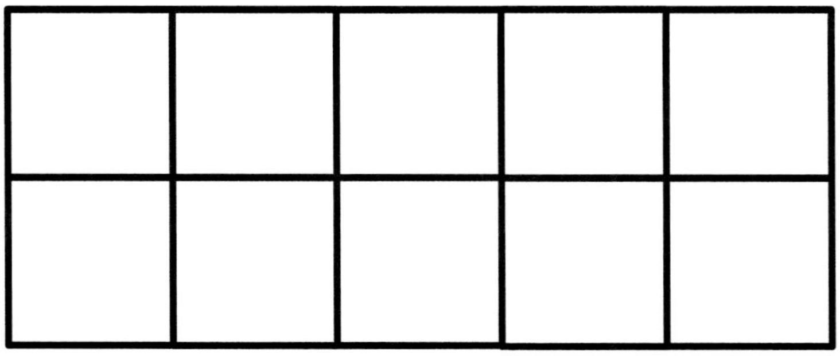

# WORD SHAPES

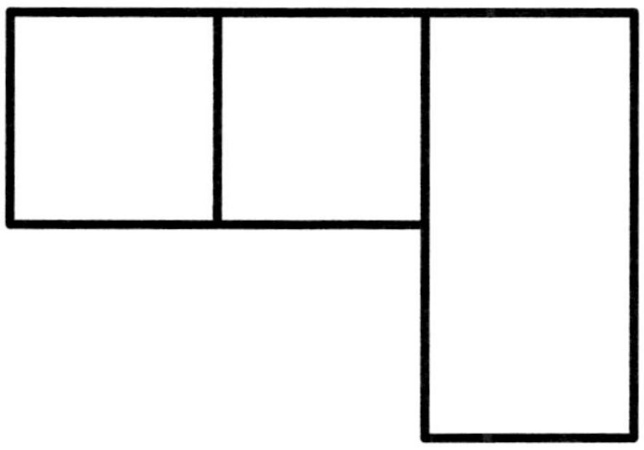

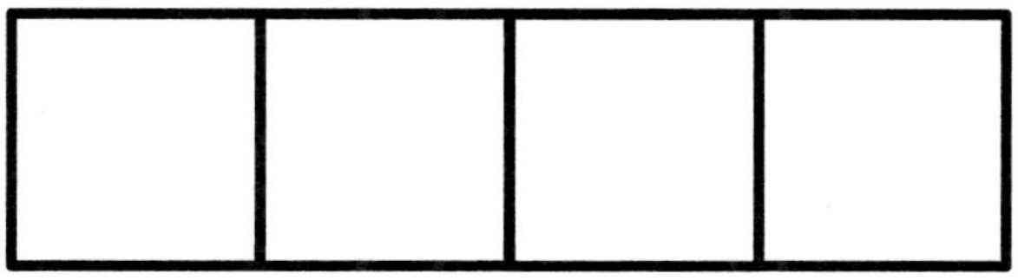

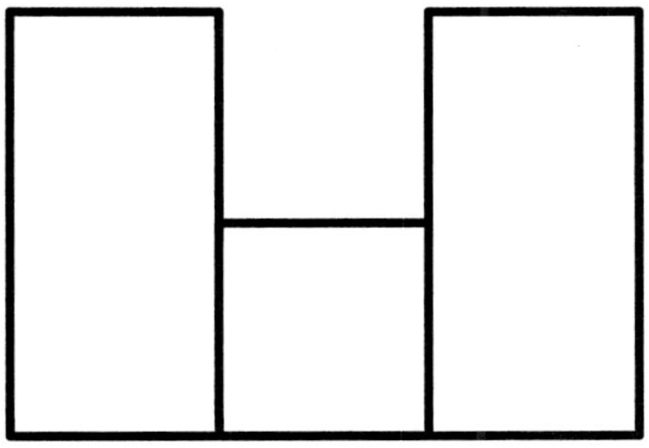

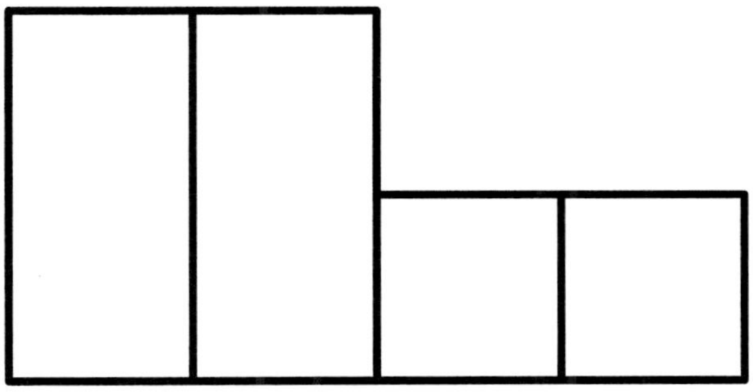

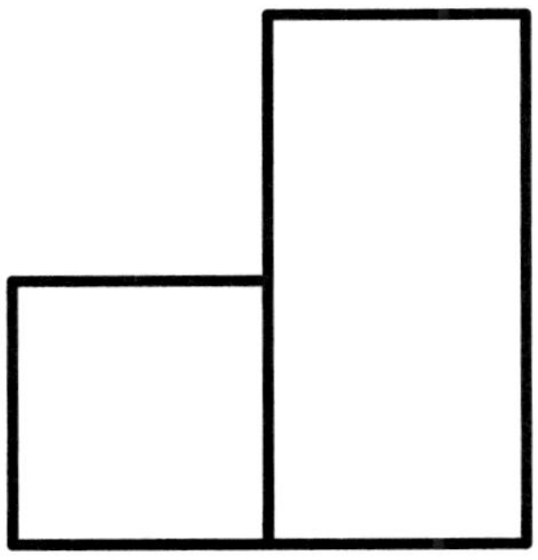

**REJECT ROLLS**

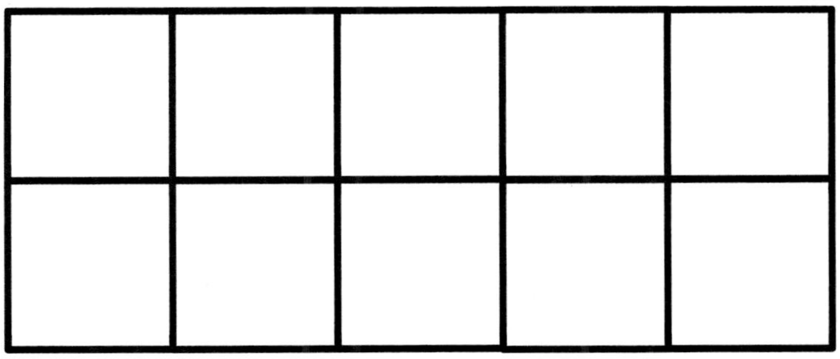

# WORD SHAPES

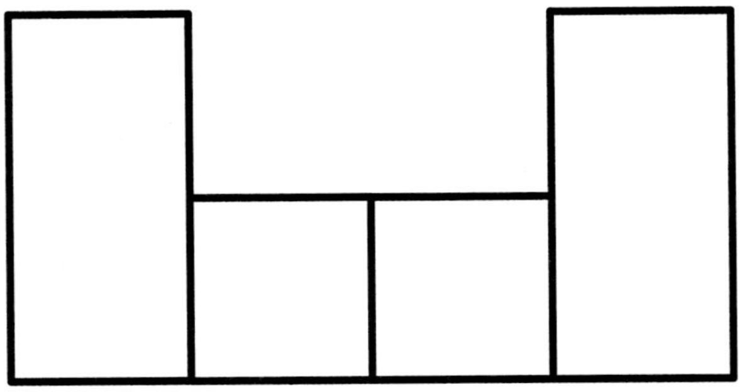

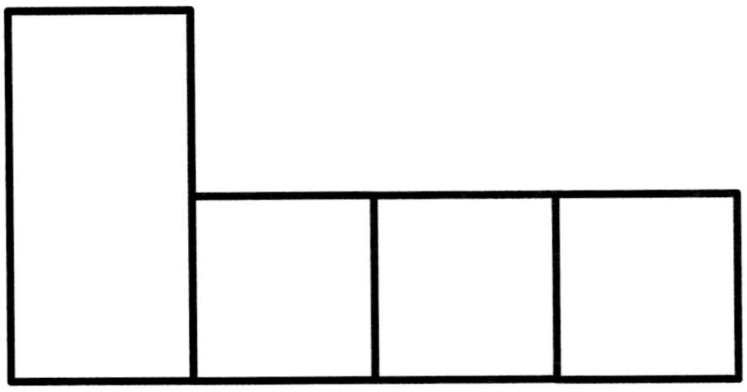

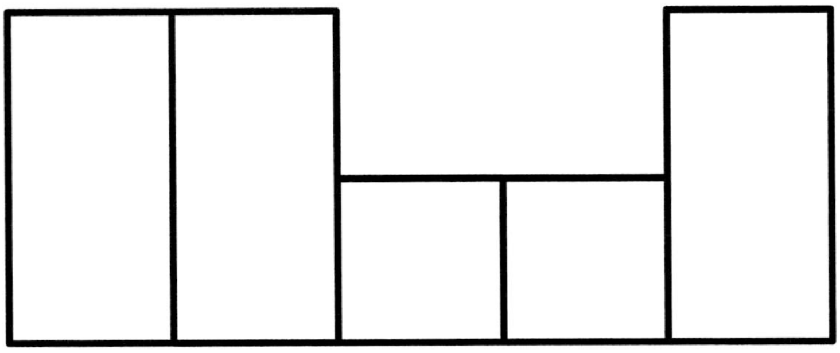

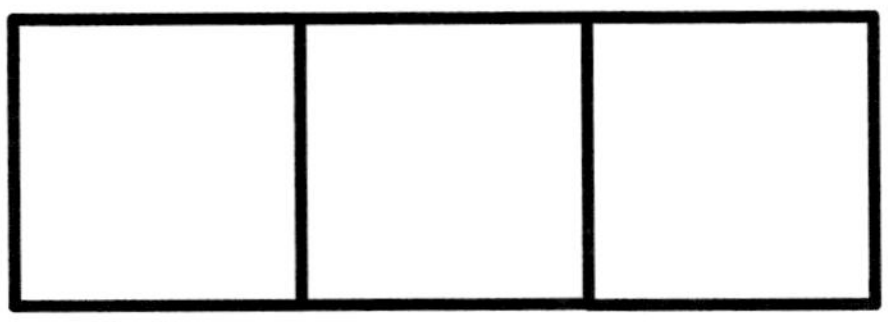

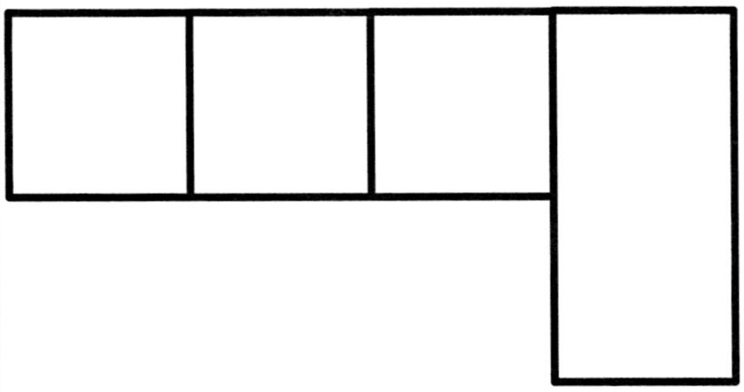

**REJECT ROLLS**

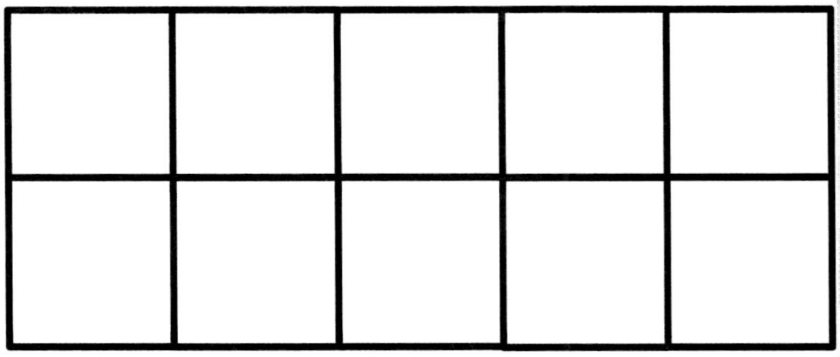

# LETTER LADDERS

**LEVEL:** grade 3 and up

**SKILLS:** learning suffixes

**PLAYERS:** 2

**EQUIPMENT:** one thirty-sided alphabet die, one gameboard per player (see black line master), letter tiles (if available) or pencil

**GOAL:** to be the player with the most correctly spelled words

## GETTING STARTED:

Players alternate rolling the die and calling the letters out loud. Both players may choose to use any letter and place it into any space on their gameboard. Players may reject ten rolls along the way. The rejected rolls are recorded in the appropriate spaces on the gameboard. If a player rolls a ☆ players may select any letter of their choice and record it anywhere on their gameboard. Once a letter is recorded into any space, it cannot be changed or erased.

***EXAMPLE:***

| | | | | | | | |
|---|---|---|---|---|---|---|---|
| q | u | i | c | k | l | y | 7 points |
| | s | l | o | w | l | y | 6 points |
| | | c | u | r | l | y | 5 points |
| | | | o | n | l | y | 4 points |
| | | | | f | l | y | 3 points |
| | | | | | | | Total 25 points |

REJECTS

| | | | | |
|---|---|---|---|---|
| | | | | |
| | | | | |

## VARIATION:

See the black line master for other ladders! Also try prefixes <u>re</u>, <u>un</u>, <u>co</u>, <u>de</u>, <u>sub</u>.

## *TEACHING TIP:*

Building word families, i.e. words ending in "ly", helps establish an understanding of common letter combinations. Teaching by using groups of words that share a spelling pattern helps students make connections.

# LETTER LADDERS

| | | | | | | | |
|---|---|---|---|---|---|---|---|
| | | | | | l | y | 7 points |
| | | | | | l | y | 6 points |
| | | | | | l | y | 5 points |
| | | | | | l | y | 4 points |
| | | | | | l | y | 3 points |

**REJECT ROLLS**

| | | | | |
|---|---|---|---|---|
| | | | | |
| | | | | |

# LETTER LADDERS

**ness = "state of"**

| | | | | | | | | | |
|---|---|---|---|---|---|---|---|---|---|
| | | | | | **n** | **e** | **s** | **s** | 9 points |
| | | | | | **n** | **e** | **s** | **s** | 8 points |
| | | | | | **n** | **e** | **s** | **s** | 7 points |
| | | | | | **n** | **e** | **s** | **s** | 6 points |

**REJECT ROLLS**

| | | | | |
|---|---|---|---|---|
| | | | | |
| | | | | |

# LETTER LADDERS

**able = "can do"**

| | | | | | | | | |
|---|---|---|---|---|---|---|---|---|
| | | | | a | b | l | e | 8 points |
| | | | | a | b | l | e | 7 points |
| | | | | a | b | l | e | 6 points |
| | | | | a | b | l | e | 5 points |

**REJECT ROLLS**

| | | | | |
|---|---|---|---|---|
| | | | | |
| | | | | |

# LETTER LADDERS

**ment = "state of"**

| | | | | | | | | | | |
|---|---|---|---|---|---|---|---|---|---|---|
| | | | | | | **m** | **e** | **n** | **t** | 10 points |
| | | | | | | **m** | **e** | **n** | **t** | 9 points |
| | | | | | | **m** | **e** | **n** | **t** | 8 points |
| | | | | | | **m** | **e** | **n** | **t** | 7 points |

**REJECT ROLLS**

| | | | | |
|---|---|---|---|---|
| | | | | |
| | | | | |

# LETTER LADDERS

| | | | | | | | | | | |
|---|---|---|---|---|---|---|---|---|---|---|
| | | | | | | | | | | 10 points |
| | | | | | | | | | | 9 points |
| | | | | | | | | | | 8 points |
| | | | | | | | | | | 7 points |
| | | | | | | | | | | 6 points |
| | | | | | | | | | | 5 points |
| | | | | | | | | | | 4 points |
| | | | | | | | | | | 3 points |

**REJECT ROLLS**

| | | | | |
|---|---|---|---|---|
| | | | | |
| | | | | |

**Other ladders to try:**

| | | |
|---|---|---|
| -tion | -ful | -less |
| -est | -er | -ous |
| -ize | -ness | -ing |
| -ied | -ed | |

**Plurals:**

-s -es -ies

# COMPOUND SNAP

**LEVEL:** grade 2 and up

**SKILLS:** recognizing compound words

**PLAYERS:** 2

**EQUIPMENT:** one thirty-sided alphabet die

**GOAL:** to be the first player to name a compound word beginning with the letter indicated

## GETTING STARTED:

Players alternate rolling the die and identifying the letter. If a ☆ is rolled, the die is re-rolled. Players now race to be the first player to give a correct compound word starting with that letter.

***EXAMPLE:***

Roll = K

Acceptable answers include:

kingfisher, keychain and keepsake

Players earn 2 points for saying a correct compound word before their opponent.

Players continue to alternate rolling the die. After a set period of time, the player with the most points is the winner

## VARIATION I:

Players may use an alphabetical gameboard to list and/or record their responses during the game, i.e.

| | |
|---|---|
| airplane | bedroom |
| courtyard | dogsled |
| evergreen | firehose |

The first player to fill ten compounds words in alphabetical sequence is the winner.

## VARIATION II:

Play a non-competitive variation. Allow players to spell as many compound words as possible during the allotted time. The team who correctly spells the most compound words wins.

***TEACHING TIP:***

Compound words are made up of at least two words. Each word must have its own vowel.

# COMPOUND SNAP

***SAMPLE COMPOUND WORDS:***

| | | | | |
|---|---|---|---|---|
| airplane | evergreen | jaywalk | popcorn | tablespoon |
| anyone | flagpole | keyboard | riverside | teacup |
| backup | fullback | keychain | screensaver | teapot |
| basketball | goldfish | laptop | seaside | teaspoon |
| bathroom | handbag | mailbox | shortchange | toothbrush |
| bedroom | handball | mountaintop | skateboard | townhouse |
| busboy | handlebar | nobody | somebody | undershirt |
| countertop | handstand | outside | someone | underwater |
| crybaby | handwriting | overdue | storefront | underwear |
| desktop | hotdog | overestimate | surfboard | whatever |
| dishwasher | inchworm | pancake | sweatpants | whenever |
| doorknob | inside | pinhole | sweatshirt | yardstick |

**HAVE YOUR STUDENTS KEEP ADDING TO THIS LIST**

# ANTSY ANTONYMS

**LEVEL:** grade 3 and up

**SKILLS:** identifying and spelling antonyms

**PLAYERS:** 2 or teams of 2 vs. 2

**EQUIPMENT:** one thirty-sided alphabet die, paper and pencil

**GOAL:** to correctly give an antonym pair that is different than their opponent's.

## GETTING STARTED:

Players roll the die and identify the starting letter. If a ☆ is rolled, the die is re-rolled. Both players now secretly spell an antonym pair using the appropriate letter.

***EXAMPLE:***
Roll = W

Player One secretly records "wide – narrow"

Player Two secretly records "white – black"

Once completed, players share their answers. If their antonym pairs are different and spelled correctly, players earn 2 points each. If the player's words are incorrectly spelled, no points are earned. If players have recorded the same antonym pairs, both players earn 1 point each.

Play continues for a set number of rounds. The player with the most points is the winner.

## VARIATION:

Antonym Snap – Players roll the die and identify the starting letter. The first player to correctly give an antonym pair scores a point. Bonus points can be earned for spelling the pair correctly. If a player is incorrect, their opponent may have an opportunity to verbalize and spell an antonym pair for 1 point.

***BONUS POINTS:***
If a player is able to identify a pair that *both* start with the letter rolled, they score 5 points, i.e.:

nice, nasty
massive, miniature

# SIMPLY SYNONYMS

**LEVEL:** grade 3 and up

**SKILLS:** identifying and spelling synonyms

**PLAYERS:** 2 or teams of 2 vs. 2

**EQUIPMENT:** one thirty-sided alphabet die, paper and pencil

**GOAL:** to give a word and an acceptable synonym for that word with each roll of the die

## GETTING STARTED:

Player One starts by rolling the die and identifying the starting letter. If a ☆ is rolled, the die is re-rolled. The player may choose any word beginning with this letter, but it must be a word that would have synonyms. Player Two must verbalize a synonym for Player One's word in order to earn a point. If players are playing in teams, Player One must verbalize a word to their partner and the partner must give a correct response for a point.

***EXAMPLE:***

Player One rolls R and chooses the word "rare" and Player Two gives the synonym "unusual" (older students may want to check their words using a thesaurus). If the player is correct, they earn 1 point. Bonus points may be awarded if the player can provide more than one synonym, i.e. "rare, unique, uncommon" etc.

Player Two now takes their turn rolling the die. Play continues for a set period of time. The player with the most points is the winner.

## VARIATION:

A snap variation can be played with 3 players. Players take turns rolling the die, and verbalizing a word starting with the rolled letter that would have synonyms. The remaining two players must now think of an appropriate synonym. The first player to respond with a correct synonym earns 1 point. If players respond at the same time, both players may earn a point. Play continues until all players have been the roller for an equal amount of turns. The player with the most points is the winner.

***BONUS POINTS:***

If a player is able to identify a pair that *both* start with the letter rolled, they score 5 points, i.e.:

sneaky, sly
giant, gargantuan

---

## *TEACHING TIP:*

Teach children to listen for syllables and try to represent each one – don't forget a vowel in each syllable!

---

# THINKING THESAURUS

**LEVEL:** grade 3 and up

**SKILLS:** identifying and spelling synonyms

**PLAYERS:** teams of 2 vs. 2

**EQUIPMENT:** one gameboard per team, regular die, thesaurus, pencil

**GOAL:** to correctly spell an acceptable synonym with the correct number of syllables before the other team

## GETTING STARTED:

Both teams have an identical gameboard. Gameboards can be created by the teacher or students to ensure that an appropriate challenge level is created. Some ideas for words may come from thematic units of study in all subject areas.

***SAMPLE GAMEBOARD:***

| SYNONYM | WORD |
|---|---|
| 1. | small |
| 2. | big |
| 3. | intelligent |
| 4. | fast |
| 5. | afraid |
| 6. | fierce |
| 7. | unusual |
| 8. | simple |
| 9. | nice |
| 10. | correct |

To begin play for the first round, a player rolls the die. This number indicates how many syllables the synonym for line number one (i.e., in this example: small) must be. Players use the following legend to determine the number of syllables:

| | | |
|---|---|---|
| Roll = 1, 2 or 3 | – | 1 syllable word (i.e. wee) |
| Roll = 4, 5 or 6 | – | 2 syllable word (i.e. tiny, petite) |

As soon as the die is rolled, both teams try to be the first to correctly spell an acceptable synonym. Once a team has recorded their answer they say "Thinking Thesaurus". They must spell their word correctly and also verify that the word is an acceptable synonym. A thesaurus can be used for this purpose. If a team is correct they may fill in their answer on the appropriate line of their gameboard and both teams proceed to the next line. For each new line, the die is re-rolled to determine the number of syllables. After all ten lines are finished, players count up the number of filled in words on their gameboards. The team with the most is the winner.

# THINKING THESAURUS

## VARIATION I:

Try similes:

As cold as a ______________________.
As hot as a ______________________.
As tall as a ______________________.
As smart as ______________________.
As quick as ______________________.
As poor as ______________________.

## VARIATION II:

Try antonyms:

| ANTONYM | WORD |
|---|---|
| 1. | small |
| 2. | perfect |
| 3. | wide |
| 4. | mean |
| 5. | intelligent |
| 6. | obese |
| 7. | free |
| 8. | pleasant |
| 9. | masculine |
| 10. | wealthy |

# THINKING THESAURUS

| SYNONYM | WORD |
| --- | --- |
| 1. ______________________ | ______________________ |
| 2. ______________________ | ______________________ |
| 3. ______________________ | ______________________ |
| 4. ______________________ | ______________________ |
| 5. ______________________ | ______________________ |
| 6. ______________________ | ______________________ |
| 7. ______________________ | ______________________ |
| 8. ______________________ | ______________________ |
| 9. ______________________ | ______________________ |
| 10. ______________________ | ______________________ |

# HOMONYM RIDDLES

**LEVEL:** grade 3 and up

**SKILLS:** identifying and spelling homonyms

**PLAYERS:** 2 or teams of 2 vs. 2

**EQUIPMENT:** one thirty-sided alphabet die, paper and pencil

**GOAL:** to correctly guess and spell a homonym pair

## GETTING STARTED:

Player One rolls the die and identifies the letter. Player One now uses this letter as the starting letter for the homonym pair riddle that they will give to Player Two.

***EXAMPLE:***
Player One rolls a P and chooses the homonym "PAIR/PEAR. Player One gives the following riddle to Player Two: "two of something". Player Two must now figure out the riddle and spell PAIR/PEAR. If the player is able to answer and correctly spell the homonym, they earn 1 point. If a ☆ is rolled the player may select any letter of their choice.

Players reverse roles for the next round. After a set period of time, the player with the most points wins.

***BONUS POINTS:***
If the team identifies and correctly spells a homonym triplet (such as TWO/TOO/TO or THERE/THEIR/THEY'RE), they earn 5 points.

---

## *TEACHING TIP:*

When playing in teams, have both players on Team A work on one homonym pair together.

---

***SAMPLE HOMONYM PAIRS:***

| | | | | |
|---|---|---|---|---|
| air/heir | eight/ate | lie/lye | right/write/wright | there/their/they're |
| awl/all | flee/flea | main/mane | rain/reign | two/too/to |
| bale/bail | fare/fair | mail/male | read/red | urn/earn |
| bare/bear | for/four | meat/meet | read/reed | vain/vein |
| break/brake | guilt/gilt | night/knight | sun/son | wait/weight |
| cast/caste | hair/hare | not/knot | steal/steel | wring/ring |
| carat/carrot | I'll/isle | no/know | shear/sheer | wood/would |
| cot/caught | jeans/genes | our/hour | sent/cent/scent | weigh/way |
| do/dew | key/quay | pair/pear | soul/sole | yew/ewe/you |
| dun/done | lone/loan | queue/cue | through/threw | |

# STAR WORDS

**LEVEL:** grade 1 and up

**SKILLS:** spelling simple three to five letter words

**PLAYERS:** 2

**EQUIPMENT:** one thirty-sided alphabet die, gameboard (see black line master), pencil or letter tiles (if available)

**GOAL:** to fill in the gameboard with as many correctly spelled words as possible.

## GETTING STARTED:

Players start the game with two blank stars on their gameboard. First, players fill in a vowel of their choice in the center of each star.

Player One begins by rolling the die and recording this letter into any space on their star. If a "Qu" is rolled, the player can choose to either record it in a single space or reroll the die. Players alternate rolling the die and filling in all spaces on their stars. Once both players have filled up their stars, they now begin to record as many words as possible.

***EXAMPLE:***

Player One's stars:

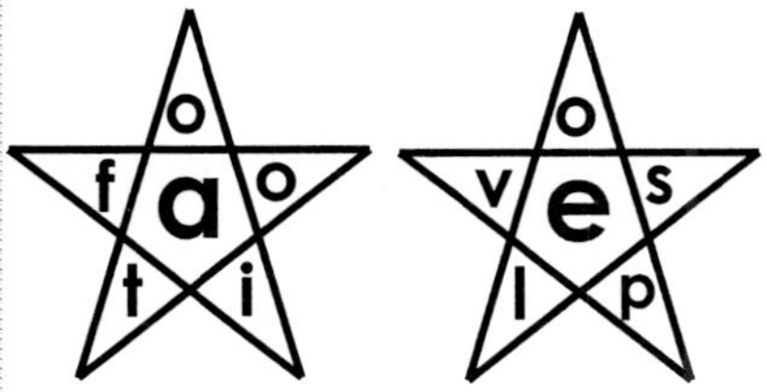


The following rules apply when building words:

- Players can only use bordering or connecting "spaces" of their star when building words
  In the above example: **fat** counts
  **it** counts
  **if** does not count
  **foot** does not count, as the **o**'s are not bordering **t**
- Words can be of any length.
- Letters cannot be used twice. If that letter has been rolled and recorded in two spaces of that star, then it can appear in the word twice.
- If a word can be duplicated, it can only be recorded and scored once.
- Plurals are allowed.

Players score one point per letter in each correctly spelled word. The player with the most points is the winner.

# STAR WORDS

***EXAMPLE:***

**Star One:**

**of fat**
**it aft**
**at oaf**
**oat**

**TOTAL:**
**18 points**

**Star Two:**

**set let**
**pest vest**
**pet lest**
**vet let's**
**step pets**

**TOTAL:**
**36 points**

**ROUND TOTAL: 54 points**

# STAR WORDS

## PLAYER ONE

**TOTAL POINTS: ______**

## PLAYER TWO

**TOTAL POINTS: ______**

# LET'TER ROLL

**LEVEL:** grade 2 and up

**SKILLS:** solitaire - 2

**PLAYERS:** creating words with a minimum of three letters

**EQUIPMENT:** one thirty-sided alphabet die, paper and pencil, gameboard (see black line master) letter tiles (if available)

**GOAL:** to create as many words as possible using letters which have been placed into a "letter bank"

## GETTING STARTED:

To begin, players build their letter bank by rolling the die twenty times and recording each roll, or alternatively taking tiles to build the letter bank. If the same letter is rolled a second time, it must be recorded again, or a duplicate tile placed into the bank. After the twenty rolls have been completed, each player looks at the letters and begins to create as many different words as possible. Each single letter may only be used once per word unless it appears twice in the letter bank, i.e. to spell "glass", s must have been rolled twice. If no vowels are rolled, players may select any two vowels and add them to their letter bank.

***EXAMPLE:***

LETTER BANK

| | | | | | | |
|---|---|---|---|---|---|---|
| k | r | s | a | m | j | |
| p | l | o | s | h | g | t |
| t | v | d | e | c | a | b |

If a ☆ is rolled a player may choose any letter to record in their letter bank.

Player One builds some of the following words: place, lace, please, lost, jog, glass, starve, cab cost.

After a set period of time, each player counts up the number of words created. The player with the most words wins.

## VARIATION I:

Players count up the letters in each word. A 3-letter word earns 3 points, a 4-letter word earns 4 points, a 5-letter word earns 5 points, and a 6+ letter word earns 10 points.

## VARIATION II:

Players earn BONUS POINTS for rhyming words, i.e. double points would be earned for **cost** and **lost**. (4 + 4 = 8 x 2 = 16 points)

# LET'TER ROLL

## VARIATION III:

Players earn 10 additional bonus points for creating meaningful sentences. Each new sentence must contain at least four different words from those previously created.

***EXAMPLE:***

LETTER BANK

| | | | | | | |
|---|---|---|---|---|---|---|
| x | u | y | e | p | d | |
| f | k | s | v | c | h | a |
| t | j | z | h | i | e | i |

1. the
2. ship
3. fade
4. is
5. hazy
6. six
7. fix
8. hive
9. key
10. five
11. jive
12. sheet
13. sheep
14. The six sheep eat chives.
15. fat
16. sat
17. hat
18. sky
19. The sky is hazy.

### *TEACHING TIP:*

This game may be introduced as a whole class activity where the teacher records the twenty rolls and prints the letters on chart paper on the chalkboard. During free time or teacher directed time, students may work cooperatively in teams or individually to create their words. This activity may continue for several days and scores are accumulated and determined at the end of the week.

# LET'TER ROLL

## Letter Bank

| | | | | | | | | | |
|---|---|---|---|---|---|---|---|---|---|
| | | | | | | | | | |
| | | | | | | | | | |

| 3-Letter Words = 3 points each | 4-Letter Words = 4 points each | 5-Letter Words = 5 points each | 6-Letter Words = 6 points each | Rhyming Pairs |
|---|---|---|---|---|
| | | | | |
| Total Words ☐ x 3 = ☐ | Total Words ☐ x 4 = ☐ | Total Words ☐ x 5 = ☐ | Total Words ☐ x 6 = ☐ | |
| Sentences (10 points each): | | | | |

# WORD BLAST

**LEVEL:** grade 3 and up

**SKILLS:** spelling simple to complex words

**PLAYERS:** 2 – 4

**EQUIPMENT:** one thirty-sided alphabet die, one gameboard per player (see black line master), pencil, letter tiles (if available)

**GOAL:** to be the first player to use all the letters on their grid by spelling new words

## GETTING STARTED:

To begin, players alternate rolling the alphabet die and building identical gameboards, i.e. the first letter rolled is a B and all players record this letter in the first square in the top row of their grid. If after twenty rolls a vowel has not been rolled, players agree on one single vowel that can be recorded as well. Once the boards have been filled in with letters, the players sit back to back and say "Blast Off". The spelling portion of the game begins as players try to use all the letters in their grid while creating a list of words. A player cannot use the same letter twice in a word unless it appears in the gameboard twice. Letters can be used in more than one word. All of the letters must be used at least once in order to win. When a player crosses off their last letter used to create a word, they say "Word Blast" and the game ends.

***EXAMPLE:***

| | | | | |
|---|---|---|---|---|
| b | s | a | r | f |
| g | w | x | d | n |
| c | e | j | o | t |
| u | y | r | h | z |

A winning list of words could include:

| | | | |
|---|---|---|---|
| oxen | gaze | frown | cow |
| joy | burst | had | |

## VARIATION:

In addition to using every letter in the gameboard, to win the round, a player must also construct a sentence using some or all of the words created in their list.

# WORD BLAST

| | | | | |
|---|---|---|---|---|
| | | | | |
| | | | | |
| | | | | |
| | | | | |

**WORDS**

| | | | | |
|---|---|---|---|---|
| | | | | |
| | | | | |
| | | | | |
| | | | | |

**WORDS**

# BRAINSTORMERS

**LEVEL:** grade 3 and up

**SKILLS:** brainstorming, spelling simple to complex words

**PLAYERS:** 2 or teams of 2 vs. 2

**EQUIPMENT:** one thirty-sided alphabet die, gameboard (see black line master), pencil

**GOAL:** to fill the board with words that fit the rolled category and starting letter, and accumulate the most points.

## GETTING STARTED:

Player or Team One rolls the die to determine the brainstorming category for the round. The die is rolled a second time to determine the starting letter for a word that fits the category. If a ☆ is rolled, the die is re-rolled.

***CATEGORIES:***

A = ANIMALS
B = BLUE OR BIG THINGS
C = COUNTRIES OR CITIES
D = DINOSAURS OR DOGS
E = ENVIRONMENT
F = FAIRY TALE WORDS OR FOOD
G = GARDEN OR GARAGE THINGS
H = THINGS FOUND IN THE HOME
I = INSECTS OR ICKY THINGS
J = THINGS THAT JUMP, JIGGLE OR JINGLE
K = THINGS FOUND IN KITCHENS
L = LOUD OR LIGHT THINGS
M = MUSICAL THINGS
N = NIGHT TIME THINGS
O = ORANGE THINGS
P = PEOPLE'S NAMES
Q = QUICK OR QUIET THINGS
R = ROUND THINGS
S = SCHOOL OR SPORT THINGS
T = TALL OR TINY THINGS
U = UNDER THE SEA
V = VEGETABLES OR VEHICLES
W = WHITE OR WOODEN THINGS
X = ANY WORD WITH AN X IN IT
Y = YELLOW THINGS
Z = THINGS FOUND IN A ZOO

# BRAINSTORMERS

***EXAMPLE:***
Roll One = B, blue or big things

Roll Two = M, starting letter

Player One spells "monsters" because monsters are big and they begin with M, and records it onto their gameboard.

If correctly spelled, Player One scores 1 point per letter. Monsters = 8 points. If a player cannot think of a word, they take a blank space and do not score any points.

BRAINSTORMERS

| | | |
|---|---|---|
| **MONSTERS** (Big Things) | **TYRANNOSAURUS** (Dinosaurs) | **JAPAN** (Countries) |
| **KIWI** (Round Things) | **QUILL** (Light Things) | **TOMATO** (Food) |
| **BANJO** (Musical Things) | **NOON HOUR** (School Things) | **LIQUID** (Environment) |
| **PANDA** (Animals) | **TIGER** (Zoo) | **AIR** (Night) |

Player Two then takes their turn and rolls both dice to generate a new category and starting letter.

Players continue to alternate turns until one player fills in their gameboard. The player with the most points wins.

## VARIATION I:
To decrease the difficulty, have players verbalize instead of spell a word that falls into the category beginning with a specific letter

## VARIATION II:
Team Competitive Play – The first team to find a word can spell it and place it into their gameboard. If it is not spelled correctly, the opposing team may try. The first team to fill in all spaces with correctly spelled words is the winner.

# BRAINSTORMERS

## BRAINSTORMERS

| | | |
|---|---|---|
| | | |
| | | |
| | | |
| | | |

## BRAINSTORMERS

| | | |
|---|---|---|
| | | |
| | | |
| | | |
| | | |

# KEEP IT GOING

**LEVEL:** grade 3 and up

**SKILLS:** brainstorming, spelling simple to complex words

**PLAYERS:** teams of 2 vs. 2

**EQUIPMENT:** one thirty-sided alphabet die, paper and pencil

**GOAL:** to verbalize twenty-six words beginning with the letters of the alphabet in sequence that fit into the selected category

## GETTING STARTED:

Players refer to the categories on p. 59 and roll the alphabet die to select the category for that round. If a ☆ is rolled, the die is re-rolled. The goal of the game is to verbalize twenty-six words beginning with the letters of the alphabet in sequence that fit into the selected category.

Team One rolls an F and names the category “fairy tale” and/or “food”. Players on Team One alternate verbalizing words that fit either category beginning with the letter A though Z

***EXAMPLE:***

| PLAYER ONE | PLAYER TWO |
|---|---|
| apple | banana |
| cantaloupe | doughnut |
| eggplant | fairies |
| goblins | ham |
| STOP | |

If a player hesitates for ten or more seconds, their play is over and they earn 1 point for each correct answer. In the above example, Team One would earn 8 points.

While Team One is verbalizing their answers, team two may also earn points by correctly spelling any or all of the words on Team One’s list. They score 2 points for each correctly spelled word.

Team Two begins their turn by rolling a letter to select a new category, i.e. Roll = S and players name the category “school” or “supermarket”. Play continues for a set period of time or until one team earns 75 points.

# KEEP IT GOING

***EXAMPLE:***
Roll = S "school or supermarket"

| PLAYER ONE | PLAYER TWO |
|---|---|
| Adding | Books |
| Cashier | Desk |
| Encyclopedia | Fruit |
| Gym | History |
| Ice cream | Juice |
| Ketchup | Library |
| Math | Noon hour |
| Office | Produce |
| Quiet | Recess |
| Science | Times table |
| Uniform | Vice Principal |
| Washroom | Xylophone |
| Yard | Ziplock bags |

## *TEACHING TIP:*

As the teams verbalize the words, they may also want to keep in mind some game strategy. For instance, they may choose to verbalize "encyclopedia" rather than eggs because encyclopedia is much more difficult to spell and lessens the opportunity for the "spelling opposition" team to earn 2 points.

An extra player may be appointed as the timer to assist both teams. The timer would be responsible for monitoring the response time and the accuracy of the given words.

# PUZZLE SPELL

**LEVEL:** grade 3 and up

**SKILLS:** spelling and creating words

**PLAYERS:** solitaire, 2 or teams of 2 vs. 2

**EQUIPMENT:** one thirty-sided alphabet die, one gameboard per player (see black line master), calculator, letter tiles (if available), paper and pencil.

**GOAL:** to earn the most points with correctly spelled words

## GETTING STARTED:

Each player needs their own gameboard.

Player One rolls and places the letter rolled in any one square. A player may not erase the letter after it has been recorded. If a ☆ is rolled, a player may choose any letter of their choice to record in their puzzle. Players alternate rolling the die and placing their letters into their gameboard.

Each player is allowed five reject rolls. If a player rolls any letter and chooses not to use this letter, it is recorded as a reject roll. That player would have four reject rolls left. The player then re-rolls a new letter.

Each player is also allowed five double roll spaces. If a player rolls a letter they would like to place in two different spaces, they may do so, i.e., rolls an S and places this in two different spaces. That player has four double chances left.

When a player has filled in all their puzzle spaces with letters the rolling for that player is over. Players now hunt for correctly spelled words in their puzzle. Each letter of the correctly spelled word is equal to the face value of the square. The player with the most points is the winner.

# PUZZLE SPELL

***EXAMPLE:***

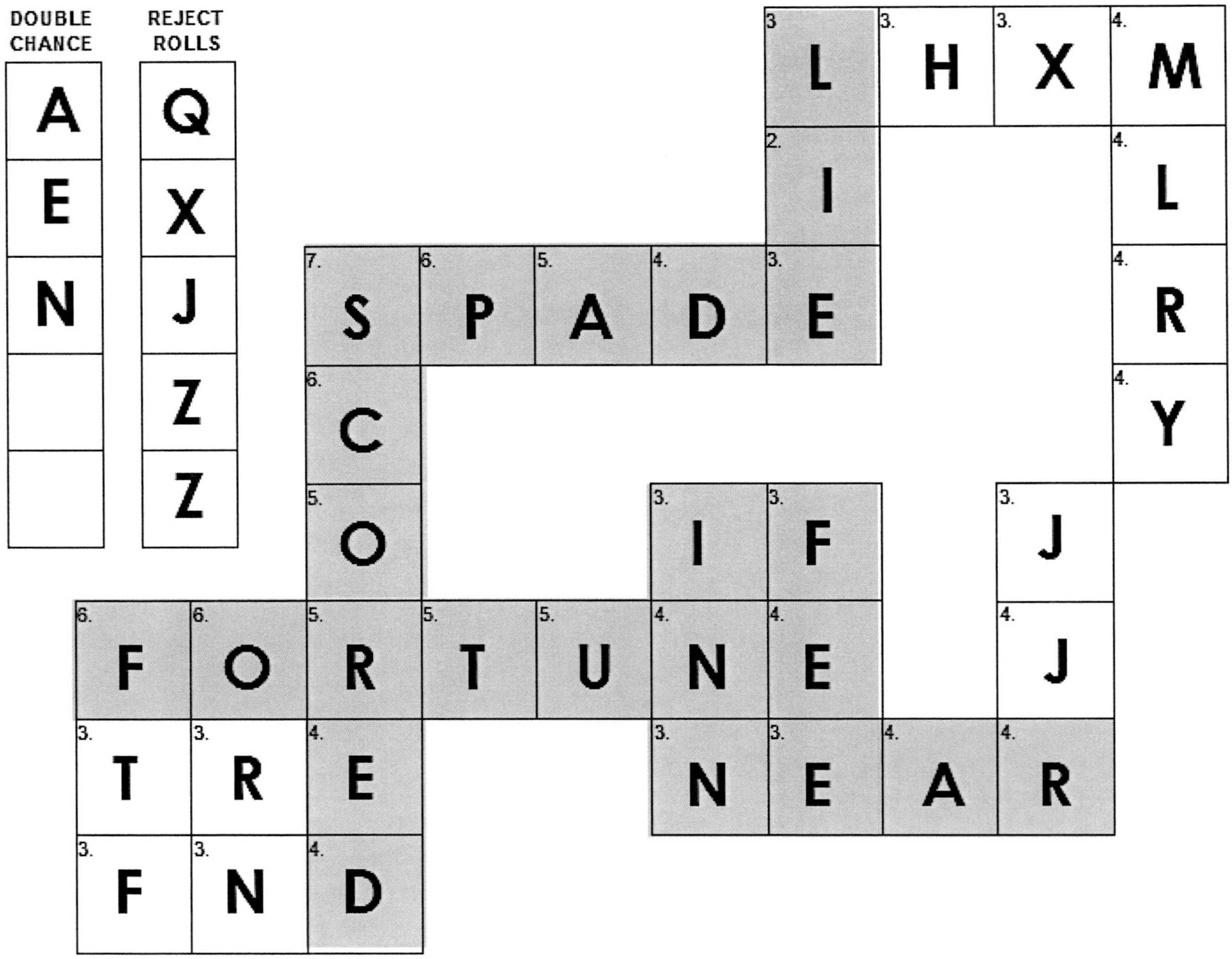


| WORD | POINTS |
|---|---|
| spade | 25 |
| inn | 10 |
| fortune | 35 |
| near | 14 |
| scored | 31 |
| lie | 8 |
| if | 6 |
| fee | 10 |

**TOTAL POINTS: 139**

# PUZZLE SPELL

DOUBLE CHANCE

REJECT ROLLS

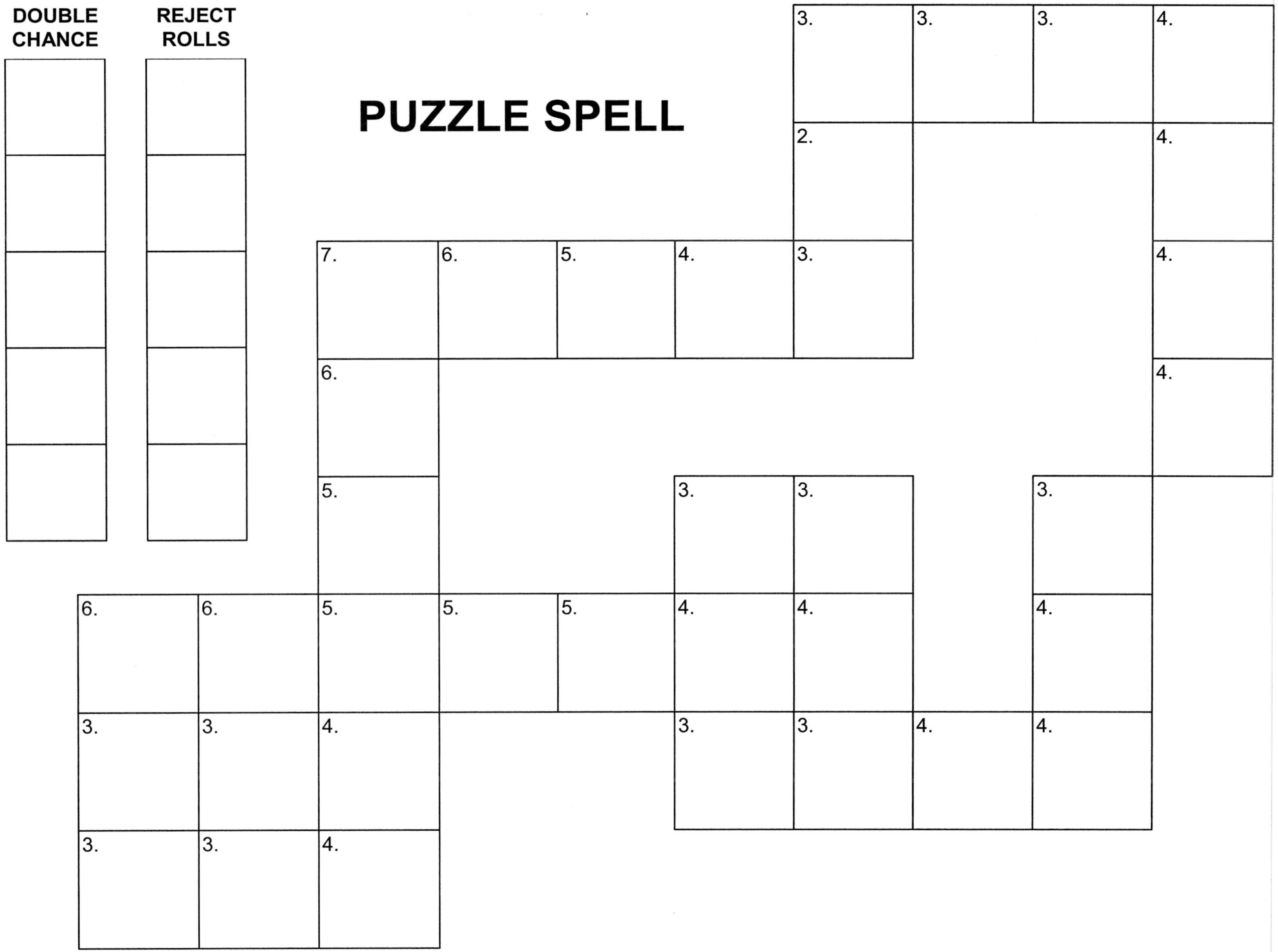

# "SPACEY" SPELLING

**LEVEL:** grade 3 and up

**SKILLS:** word recognition, spelling simple words

**PLAYERS:** solitaire or 2

**EQUIPMENT:** one thirty-sided alphabet die, one gameboard per player (see black line master), pencil

**GOAL:** to spell the most words using the letters in your gameboard

## GETTING STARTED:

Each player needs their own gameboard. Words must be created using the letters in horizontal, vertical or diagonal sequence. Both forward and backward directions are acceptable (see example). To begin, players record any two vowels into any two spaces of their choice. Players now roll to fill in each row of their gameboards starting in the first square of the top row and ending in the last square of the bottom row. If a ☆ is rolled the player may choose any letter to fill in the square.

Once the grid has been completely filled in, the players may begin to look for any correctly spelled words with a minimum of two letters. The players circle the words and spell them in list form in the space provided on the gameboard.

The player with the most correctly spelled words wins.

***EXAMPLE:***

| | | | | | |
|---|---|---|---|---|---|
| T | R | D | B | O | X |
| C | L | I | N | F | E |
| K | P | K | J | O | P |
| Q | S | K | R | N | Z |
| L | O | L | I | P | O |

| | |
|---|---|
| OR | OF OF |
| BOX | LIP |
| IN | ON ON ON |
| NO NO NO | KID |
| SO | |

# "SPACEY" SPELLING

WORDS

WORDS

# GRID LOCKED

**LEVEL:** grade 3 and up

**SKILLS:** spelling simple to complex words

**PLAYERS:** 2 or teams of 2 vs. 2

**EQUIPMENT:** one thirty-sided alphabet die, one gameboard per player or team (see black line master), pencil

**GOAL:** to make as many 2-, 3-, 4-, 5- and 6-letter words as possible.

## GETTING STARTED:

Players alternate rolling the die and saying the letter out loud. Both players place this letter anywhere in their grid, but once it is placed it cannot be changed or erased. If a player rolls a ☆ both players may choose any letter of their choice.

Players continue rolling the die until the gameboards are complete. After the rolls are completed, players figure out how many 2-, 3-, 4-, 5-, and 6-letter words have been correctly spelled in their grid either horizontally, vertically or diagonally.

Players score 2 points for a 2-letter word, 3 points for a 3-letter word, etc.

---

### *TEACHING TIP:*

It may be easier for players to list the words correctly spelled in their gameboard as they are created. Players may wish to circle them on the grid during the play of the game.

---

### *TEACHING TIP:*

As players place their letters, have them keep in mind the strategy of looking for small words that make up a larger one, i.e., “star” is composed of “star”, “tar”, “tar” and backwards “rat” and “rats”!

# GRID LOCKED

***EXAMPLE:***

| | | | | | |
|---|---|---|---|---|---|
| D | E | R | A | S | E |
| N | Z | K | H | T | L |
| A | T | Q | J | A | O |
| M | X | K | J | L | M |
| E | P | S | O | B | W |
| W | Q | U | N | E | W |

| 2-letter words | 3-letter words | 4-letter words | 5-letter words | 6-letter words |
|---|---|---|---|---|
| ON | MAN | NAME | ERASE | |
| BE | MEW | MOLE | BLAST | |
| AN | RED | LAST | | |
| AT | HAM | | | |
| HA | SOB | | | |
| AX | ARE | | | |
| NO | NEW | | | |
| UP | | | | |
| | | | | |
| | | | | |

# GRID LOCKED

| | | | | | |
|---|---|---|---|---|---|
| | | | | | |
| | | | | | |
| | | | | | |
| | | | | | |
| | | | | | |
| | | | | | |

| 2-letter words | 3-letter words | 4-letter words | 5-letter words | 6-letter words |
|---|---|---|---|---|
| ______ | ______ | ______ | ______ | ______ |
| ______ | ______ | ______ | ______ | ______ |
| ______ | ______ | ______ | ______ | ______ |
| ______ | ______ | ______ | ______ | ______ |
| ______ | ______ | ______ | ______ | ______ |
| ______ | ______ | ______ | ______ | ______ |
| ______ | ______ | ______ | ______ | ______ |
| ______ | ______ | ______ | ______ | ______ |
| ______ | ______ | ______ | ______ | ______ |
| ______ | ______ | ______ | ______ | ______ |

# PARTS OF SPEECH PIZZAZZ

**LEVEL:** grade 4 and up

**SKILLS:** identifying parts of speech, spelling

**PLAYERS:** 2 or teams of 2 vs. 2

**EQUIPMENT:** one thirty-sided alphabet die, one gameboard per player (see black line master), paper and pencil.

**GOAL:** to be the first player to fill in all spaces of their gameboard with correctly spelled words

## GETTING STARTED:

Players use the following legend for the regular die roll:

1 = noun
2 = verb
3 = adjective
4 = adverb
5 = preposition/interjection
6 = players choose any part of speech

Player One rolls the alphabet die and identifies the starting letter for their word. If a ☆ is rolled the player may choose the letter of their choice. The regular die is rolled to indicate the type of word the player must spell. i.e., Roll = M and 3.

Player One must spell an adjective beginning with the letter M. Some possible words might include: mauve, merry, mischievous, etc.

Player One must correctly spell their chosen word before filling it into the appropriate space on their gameboard. If they cannot spell it, or cannot think of an appropriate word, then nothing is filled in. Player Two now takes their turn. Players continue to alternate turns. The first player to fill in their gameboard is the winner.

---

### *TEACHING TIP:*

An interjection is a word that shows an exclamation of surprise, sorrow, delight or some other emotion, i.e., Oh! Ah! Hurray!

---

# PARTS OF SPEECH PIZZAZZ

| NOUN | VERB | ADJECTIVE | ADVERB | PREPOSITION/ INTERJECTION |
|---|---|---|---|---|
| | | | | |
| | | | | |
| | | | | |
| | | | | |

| NOUN | VERB | ADJECTIVE | ADVERB | PREPOSITION/ INTERJECTION |
|---|---|---|---|---|
| | | | | |
| | | | | |
| | | | | |
| | | | | |

| NOUN | VERB | ADJECTIVE | ADVERB | PREPOSITION/ INTERJECTION |
|---|---|---|---|---|
| | | | | |
| | | | | |
| | | | | |
| | | | | |

# SPEEDY PARTS OF SPEECH

**LEVEL:** grade 4 and up

**SKILLS:** identifying parts of speech: verbs, nouns, adjectives, spelling words

**PLAYERS:** 2 or teams of 2 vs. 2

**EQUIPMENT:** one thirty-sided alphabet die, gameboard (see black line master), pencil

**GOAL:** to be the first player to fill in all spaces of their gameboard with correctly spelled words

## GETTING STARTED:

Each player needs their own gameboard. Player One rolls the die. Both players now race to verbalize either a verb, noun or adjective starting with that letter, i.e., Player One rolls an R and Player Two verbalizes "ran – verb". Player Two must now correctly spell that word before filling it into the appropriate space on their gameboard. If the word is spelled correctly it is recorded and a new letter is rolled. If the player does not spell the word correctly, then their opponent has the opportunity to verbalize and spell a word starting with the letter rolled. If successful, they fill this word into their gameboard and a new letter is rolled for the next round. If a ☆ is rolled, players re-roll the die.

Players continue to alternate rolling the die. The first player to complete their gameboard is the winner.

***EXAMPLE:***

| VERBS | NOUNS | ADJECTIVES |
|---|---|---|
| RAN | BOAT | YELLOW |
| KICKED | OLIVE | TIGHT |
| FLEW | JET | SHINY |
| CALL | MOUSE | DARK |

## VARIATION:

Non-competitive play. Players play cooperatively as teams and work together to fill in all spaces of their gameboard after only one roll of the die, i.e. an S is rolled and players must fill in all spaces of their board with words beginning with the letter S.

# SPEEDY PARTS OF SPEECH

Roll = S

| VERBS | NOUNS | ADJECTIVES |
|---|---|---|
| SLID | SOFA | SILKY |
| SKIPPED | SCHOOL | SLIMY |
| SNORED | SANDWICH | SUNNY |
| SKATED | SNAKE | STINKY |

Teams work together to complete their gameboard. Teams check each other's boards for accuracy and earn 1 point for each correctly spelled response.

## *TEACHING TIP:*

Knowing the Etymology (history of words) can help with spelling. Origin is indicated in the dictionary entry. By collecting words and putting them into word origin categories, students can make some spelling generalizations, i.e., rodeo, mosquito, pueblo.

# SPEEDY PARTS OF SPEECH

| VERBS | NOUNS | ADJECTIVES |
| --- | --- | --- |
| | | |
| | | |
| | | |
| | | |

| VERBS | NOUNS | ADJECTIVES |
| --- | --- | --- |
| | | |
| | | |
| | | |
| | | |

# ROLL 'EM ... AND ACTION

**LEVEL:** grade 4 and up

**SKILLS:** identifying verbs, spelling

**PLAYERS:** 2

**EQUIPMENT:** one thirty-sided alphabet die, gameboard (see reproducibles), paper and pencil

**GOAL:** to be the first player to fill in all the spaces on their gameboard with correctly spelled verbs

## GETTING STARTED:

Each player needs their own gameboard. Player One rolls the die. If a ☆ is rolled, the die is re-rolled. Both players now race to spell a verb starting with that letter.

When a player has spelled a word, that player calls "action" and spells their word to their opponent. If the word is a verb and is spelled correctly, it is recorded into the player's gameboard and a new letter is rolled.

If the player does not spell the word correctly, then their opponent has the opportunity to spell a word starting with the letter rolled. If successful, they fill this word into their gameboard and a new letter is rolled for the round.

Players continue alternating rolling the die. The first player to complete their gameboard is the winner.

***EXAMPLE:***

| | | | |
|---|---|---|---|
| 1. fled | 2. hoped | 3. laughed | 4. cried |
| 5. played | 6. drove | 7. danced | 8. shot |
| 9. ran | 10. studied | 11. threw | 12. skated |

## VARIATION:

Try nouns, adjectives or adverbs.

# ROLL 'EM … AND ACTION

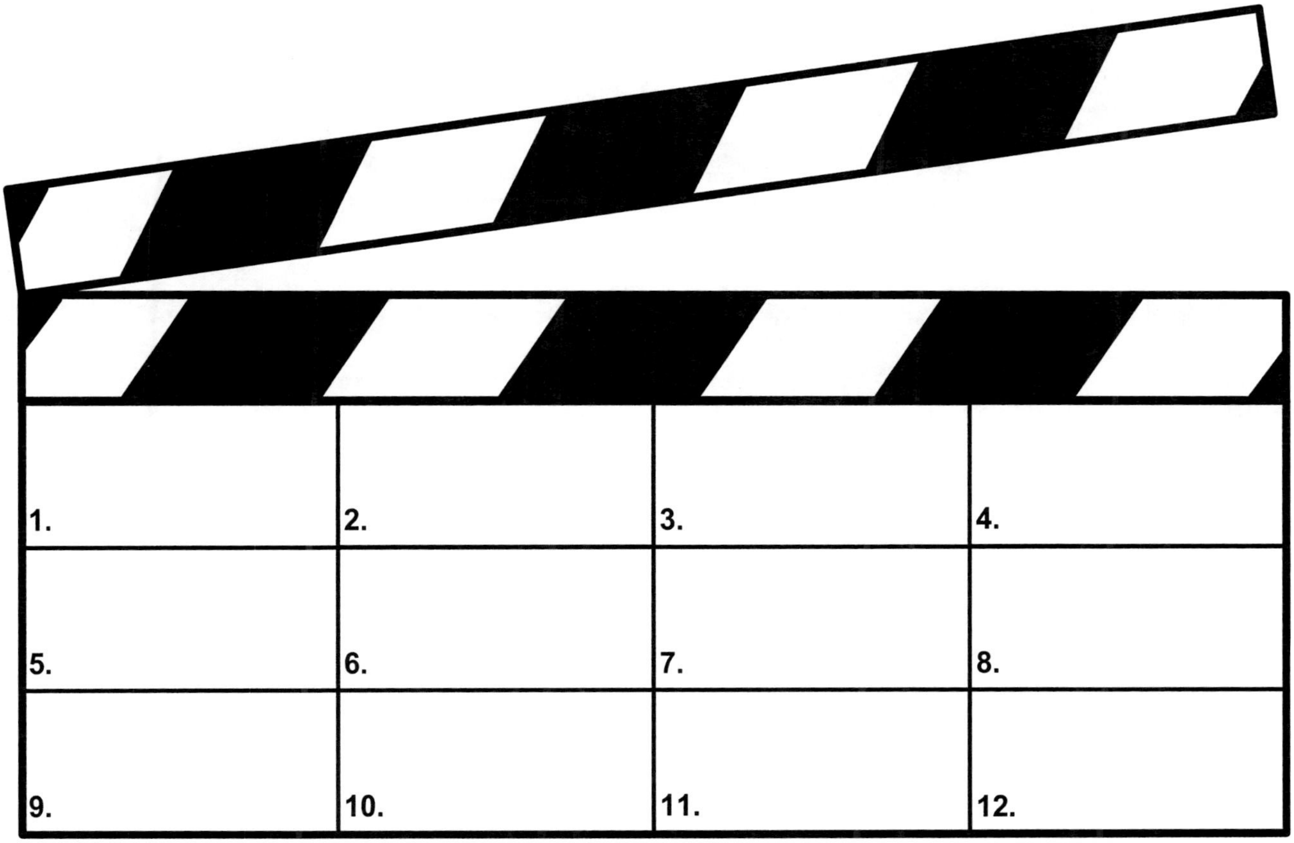


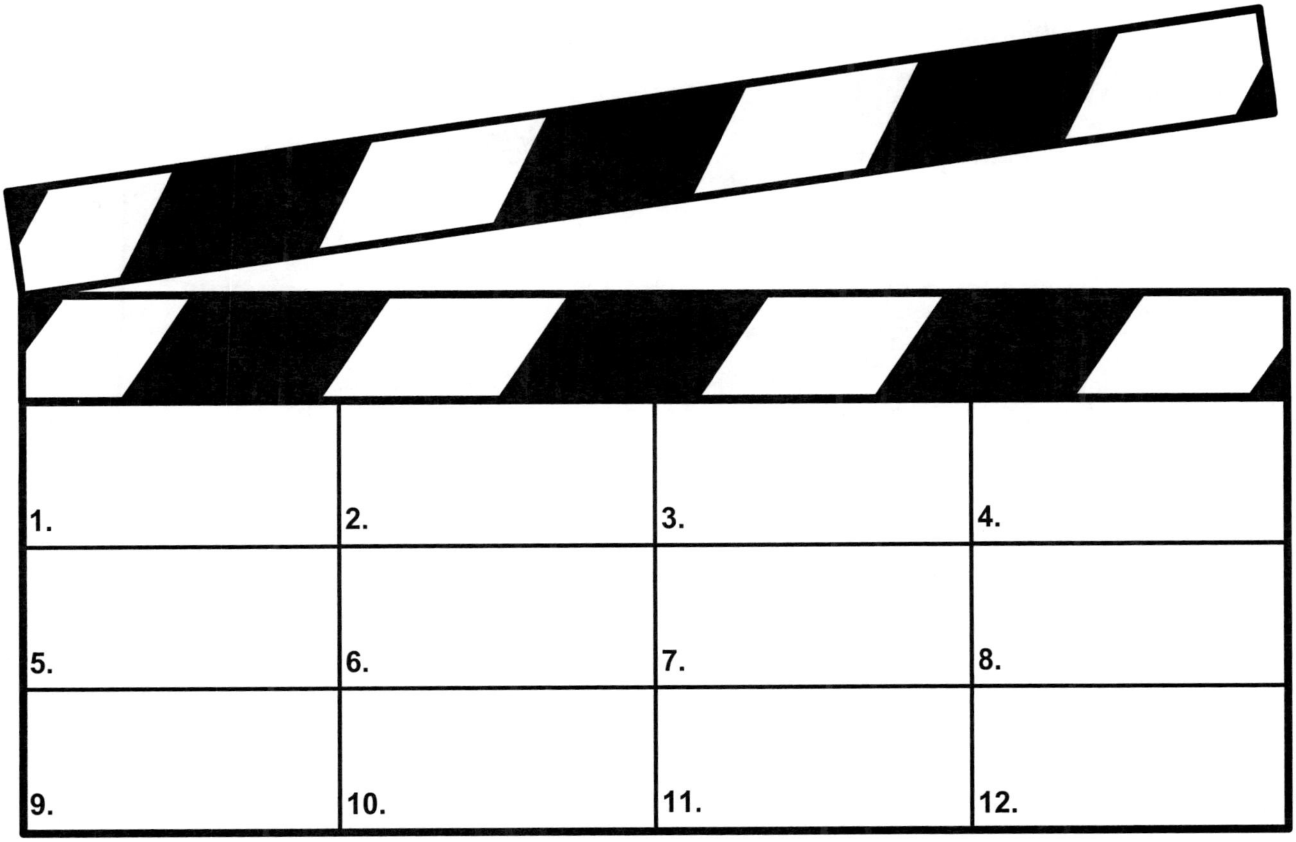

# box cars and one-eyed jacks®

## Box Cars And One-Eyed Jacks Series Include:

**Shuffling Into Math** - Kindergarten to Grade 3

**All Hands On Deck** Math Games Using Cards and Dice - Grades 1 to 9

**Dice Works** Math Games Using Special Dice - Kindergarten to Grade 9

**Rolling In The Dough** Money Games For Kids - Ages 5 to 12

**Math Attack** Math Games For Kids Using 30-Sided Dice - Kindergarten to Grade 9

**On A Roll** To Spelling And More - Kindergarten to Grade 6

**Piece It Together With Fractions** - Grades 1 to 7

**Stratedice** Games For 36 Dice - Ages 6 and Up

**Deca Dice** Math Games For Kids Using Decade Dice - Grades 1 to 9

**Radical Math** Millennium Edition - Grades 6 to 12

**Spelling Rules** With These Cool Tools - Ages 5 to 105

**Double Dare You** Amazing Math Games Using Double Dice - Ages 6 to 15

**Power Play** Place Value Games For Kids - Grades 1 to 9

**Domino Math Games** Connecting The Dots* - Ages 5 to 10

**Domino Math Games** Linking The Learning* - Ages 8 to 13

**Daily Physical Education** No Sweat For Classroom Teachers** - Kindergarten to Grade 9

**Shuffling Into Math** With Fun Family Games - Kindergarten to Grade 3

**All Hands On Deck** Fun Family Math Games - Grades 3 to 6

**Play On Words** Literacy Games - Kindergarten to Grade 4

**On A Roll To Literacy** - Kindergarten to Grade 6

**Over 250,000 Of The Books In Our Series Are Already In Classrooms**

**VISIT OUR WEBSITE boxcarsandoneeyedjacks.com TO LEARN MORE**

* Originally published by Cadamac Corp and No Sweat Education, currently published by Cadamac Corp and Box Cars And One-Eyed Jacks Inc.
** Originally published by No Sweat Education, currently published by Box Cars And One-Eyed Jacks Inc.